Ta

]

MW01489691

II. MOON CALENDAR*

*Each moon features Herbal Lore by Billie Potts
and Astrological Predictions by Gretchen Lawlor.

III. APPENDIX

 1995 9995

JANUARY

M	T	W	T	F	S	S
						1
2	3	4	5	6	7	8
9	10	11	12	13	14	15
16	17	18	19	20	21	22
23	24	25	26	27	28	29
30	31					

FEBRUARY

M	T	W	T	F	S	S
		1	2	3	4	5
6	7	8	9	10	11	12
13	14	15	16	17	18	19
20	21	22	23	24	25	26
27	28					

MARCH

M	T	W	T	F	S	S
		1	2	3	4	5
6	7	8	9	10	11	12
13	14	15	16	17	18	19
20	21	22	23	24	25	26
27	28	29	30	31		

APRIL

M	T	W	T	F	S	S
					1	2
3	4	5	6	7	8	9
10	11	12	13	14	15	16
17	18	19	20	21	22	23
24	25	26	27	28	29	30

MAY

M	T	W	T	F	S	S
1	2	3	4	5	6	7
8	9	10	11	12	13	14
15	16	17	18	19	20	21
22	23	24	25	26	27	28
29	30	31				

JUNE

M	T	W	T	F	S	S
			1	2	3	4
5	6	7	8	9	10	11
12	13	14	15	16	17	18
19	20	21	22	23	24	25
26	27	28	29	30		

JULY

M	T	W	T	F	S	S
					1	2
3	4	5	6	7	8	9
10	11	12	13	14	15	16
17	18	19	20	21	22	23
24	25	26	27	28	29	30
31						

AUGUST

M	T	W	T	F	S	S
	1	2	3	4	5	6
7	8	9	10	11	12	13
14	15	16	17	18	19	20
21	22	23	24	25	26	27
28	29	30	31			

SEPTEMBER

M	T	W	T	F	S	S
				1	2	3
4	5	6	7	8	9	10
11	12	13	14	15	16	17
18	19	20	21	22	23	24
25	26	27	28	29	30	

OCTOBER

M	T	W	T	F	S	S
						1
2	3	4	5	6	7	8
9	10	11	12	13	14	15
16	17	18	19	20	21	22
23	24	25	26	27	28	29
30	31					

NOVEMBER

M	T	W	T	F	S	S
	1	2	3	4	5
6	7	8	9	10	11	12
13	14	15	16	17	18	19
20	21	22	23	24	25	26
27	28	29	30			

DECEMBER

M	T	W	T	F	S	S
				1	2	3
4	5	6	7	8	9	10
11	12	13	14	15	16	17
18	19	20	21	22	23	24
25	26	27	28	29	30	31

There is a brokenness
          out of which comes the unbroken,
  a shatteredness out of which blooms the unshatterable.
There is a sorrow
          beyond all grief which leads to joy
and a fragility
          out of whose depths emerges strength.

There is a hollow space
          too vast for words
through which we pass with each loss,
out of whose darkness we are sanctioned into being.

      There is a cry deeper than all sound
whose serrated edges cut the heart
          as we break open
to the place inside which is unbreakable
          and whole,
      while learning to sing.

- Rashani

What Is *WE'MOON*?
A Handbook in Natural Cycles

The **We'Moon: Gaia Rhythms for Womyn** is more than an appointment book. It is a way of life! **We'Moon** is a *handbook in natural rhythm*. As we chart our days alongside other heavenly bodies, we begin to discover patterns in how we interrelate. **We'Moon** comes out of an *international womyn's culture*. Art and writings by we'moon from many lands give a glimpse of the great diversity and uniqueness of a world we create in our own image. **We'Moon** is about *womyn's spirituality* (spirit'reality). We share how we live our truth, what inspires us, how we envision our reality in connection with the whole Earth and all our relations.

We'Moon means "We of the Moon." The Moon, whose cycles run in our blood, is the original womyn's calendar. Like the Moon, we'moon circle the Earth. We are drawn to one another. We come in different shapes, colors, and sizes. We are continually transforming. With all our different hues and points of view, we are one.

We'Moon means "women." Instead of defining ourselves in relation to men, ("woman" means "wife of man" in old English; "female" is another derivative from "male"), we use the word *we'moon* to define ourselves by our primary relation to the natural sources of cosmic flow ("we of the moon"). Other terms we'moon use are: womyn, wimmin, womon, womb-one. **We'Moon** is a moon calendar for we'moon. As we'moon, we seek to be whole in ourselves, rather than dividing ourselves in half and hoping that some "other half" will complete the picture. In **We'Moon** we see the whole range of life's potential embodied by we'moon. We also do not divide the rest of the universe into sex-role stereotypes according to the heterosexual model. We see the goddess equally in the Sun and the Moon, in the Earth and the sky.

We'moon culture exists in the diversity and the oneness of our experience as we'moon. *We honor both.* We are in all cultures, coming from very different ways of life, and we have a culture of our own as we'moon, sharing a common mother root. We are glad when we'moon from many different cultures contribute art and writing. When material is borrowed from cultures other than your own, we ask that it be acknowledged and something given in return. Being conscious of our sources keeps us from engaging in the divisiveness of either *cultural appropriation* (taking what belongs to others) or *cultural fascism* (controlling creative expression). We invite every we'moon to share how the "Mother Tongue" speaks to her, with respect both for cultural integrity and individual freedom.

We'Moon look into the mirror of the sky to discover patterns in how we move here on earth. Like all native and natural earth-loving people since ancient times, we naturally assume a connection with a larger whole of which we are a part.

6

We show the natural cycles of the Moon, Sun, planets and stars, as they relate to Earth. By recording our own activities side by side with those of other heavenly bodies, we may notice what connection, if any, there is for us.

Gaia Rythms: The Earth revolves around her axis in one day; the Moon orbits around the Earth in one month (29 $^1/_5$ days); the Earth orbits around the Sun in one year. We experience each of these cycles by the alternating rhythms of day and night, waxing and waning, Summer and Winter. The Earth/Moon/Sun are our inner circle of kin in the universe. We know where we are in relation to them at all times by the dance of lights and shadows as they circle around one another.

The Eyes of Heaven: As seen from Earth, the Moon and the Sun are equal in size: "the left and right eye of Heaven," according to Hindu (Eastern) astrology. Unlike the solar-dominated calendars of Christian (Western) patriarchy, the **We'Moon** looks at our experience through both eyes at once, with stars for our third eye.

The **lunar eye** of heaven is seen each day in the phases of the Moon. *Moons/months* begin when the Moon and the Sun are conjunct at *new* or *dark Moon.* There are *thirteen Moons* (or months), with two pages of graphics and writing between to set them off. 13 is a lunar number which signifies the coming together of the Moon and Sun cycles.

The **solar eye** of heaven is given with the turning points in the Sun cycle (see "Wheel of the Year: Holy Days" p. 26). The year begins with the *nearest new Moon to Winter Solstice* (in the Northern Hemisphere), the dark time or renewal in both the Sun and Moon cycles. Solstices, Equinoxes, and the Cross-quarter days in between give the rhythm of the seasons.

The **third eye** of heaven may be seen in the stars. Astrology measures the cycles by relating the Sun, Moon, and all other planets in our universe through the *star signs.* The zodiac is how we tell time in the larger cycles of the universe – out beyond the field of light and dark.

Measuring Time and Space: Imagine a clock with many hands. The Earth is the center from which we view our universe. The Sun, Moon, and planets are like the hands of the clock. Each one has its own rate of movement through the cycle. The ecliptic, a band of sky around Earth within which all planets have their orbits, is the outer band of the clock where the numbers are. Stars along the ecliptic are grouped into constellations forming the signs of the zodiac – the twelve star signs are like the twelve numbers of the clock. They mark the movements of the planets through the 360° circle of the sky, which are like the hands on the clock of time and space.

Whole Earth Perspective: It is important to note that all natural cycles have a mirror image from a whole Earth perspective. The seasons (Summer/Winter, Spring/Fall) are always opposite in the Northern and Southern hemispheres. Day and night are at opposite times on opposite sides of the earth, East to West.

◻ *Musawa*

Survivors

Seven women from the north
Two from the south
and two from Fly Away Home
sat in circle
under Their Great Shelter
and began to weave
for We'Moon.

We all took piles
in our cross-legged
leaning back
rocking chair laps
and began to read,
at first with much spontaneous chatter,
then, in the silence of our bodies.

We read for hours
in that ten-sided house,
expanding and contracting
with the theme of our task:
surviving

The south-facing windows
stretched bigger than life.
The wind whittled down to nothing.
Not even the trees spoke.

From time to time
one or a few would get up,
go over to the table in the best of daylight,
lean or sway over the artwork
so painfully, plainly presented.

"I don't know if I don't like it
or if it just hurts me to see it,"
one woman said into the space.
Heat rising when I saw the drawing myself,
I wanted to recoil, not wanting
it to be true that
the demons we draw
are the demons
we've experienced.

Hardwood floor. Wings
rushing around the woman
in the rocking chair.
I feel her crying
in the extra breath
she draws from the room.
Pencils drop.
Later she lays in front of the fire
her head and naked torso
covered by a pink, tattered blanket.

I want to cup her feet.
I want to lay my body over hers
protecting her from
the light.
This whole time
I have been wanting
to curl my hand in a "c"
and run my thumb and fingers
down every woman's back;
the trembling fibers
are singing,
the trembling fibers
are trembling,
and even as they're snapping
the stringed instruments of our bodies
are playing a healing song.

¤ *Caroline Brumleve 1993*
We'Moon Weaving Circle,
Fly Away Home, December 7   9

CREATION OF THE MOON THEMES: SHARING OUR PROCESS

In each of the thirteen Moons, we take an aspect of the theme, **Survivors: The Healer Within.** Each Moon theme was determined by a complex *weaving* process that involved many wimmin sifting through an abundance of art and writing that was sent in, culling out the main themes, and giving feedback until the contents of the Moons started to come together in one organic whole. This year, we combined the *qualities* of cardinal, fixed, and mutable energies with the *elements* of each sign as the warp and woof of our weaving.

We asked ourselves: when the new Moon and Sun are in Aries, at the beginning of Spring, which themes would be most at home in this Moon that reflects *Cardinal Fire* energy? **Anger/Breaking Silence** seemed to be the fiery beginning place for many wimmin in healing and initiating change. When the new Moon and Sun are in the *Fixed Fire* sign of Leo, in the Summer months, the will to carry on seemed to be expressed as **Will/Wildness.** When they are in the *Mutable Fire* sign of Sagittarius, Fall gives way to Winter and we turn to the embers of our inside fires, finding **Allies/Protectors** that support transformation. And so it goes, through the other signs and seasons, qualities and elements of Gaia rhythms. Moon themes are listed in the Table of Contents.

In this fabric of many strands, we hope to honor some of the mini-cycles (as well as the larger seasonal ones) that may happen within the healing process, which is so different for everyone. Perhaps you may find teachings in the cycles of the Moon, or parallels to your journey with the branches that at first look like sticks against the sky, then begin to swell into buds, moving into another incarnation of life and selfness. As the wheel of the year turns, may we draw from the cycles of the Earth, Moon, Sun, Stars and Ourselves to illuminate our way and strengthen us on our path towards healing.

This **We'Moon** is an offering to be used in whatever way fits best for you. This is not an ordinary calendar. You may choose to relate to it on many different levels: as an appointment book with beautiful art and writing, as a guide to natural rhythms, or as a close companion on a very personal healing journey. We encourage you to be aware of your own reactions as you go, and give them the space and honor they deserve.

Creatrix Matrix (Beth, Pandora, and Musawa)

□ *Jody Turner 1993*

Introduction to the Theme:
Survivors: The Healer Within

We are using a broad definition of survivors to mean anyone who has survived deep loss, dis-ease or abuse in any form – mind or body, heart or soul. Abuse is whatever violates the Spirit of any being on any level: by overpowering, doing violence to, inflicting one being's will onto another, or dishonoring the integrity or value of any being.

Many human cultures (particularly white, Western, male-dominated cultures) have, in the last few thousand years, made quite a mess of things. Though magic, beauty, and love are constantly present and run deep, there is much pain everywhere that runs equally deep. The list of hurts is long. Human cultures that are based on such things as control, power, and money have rearranged much of the world to the liking of those in power. For example, genocide of Earth-loving cultures has been systematically carried out for the acquisition of land and her natural resources. The Earth has been ravaged in vast and countless ways. Sexual and physical abuse against wimmin and children runs rampant. People are plagued with senseless violence, and with ways of thinking that deem some "less than" oth-

ers because of race, sex, age, ability, sexual orientation, class, religion, nation, tribe, lifestyle, species... any quality that makes us different. In these cultures, we all lose; *nobody* is free from the repercussions of such oppression. We are *all* survivors of patriarchy.

As survivors, we develop strategies for protecting ourselves and living in the world in a safe way. These survival strategies are resourceful and creative means to stay alive and be as present as possible. As we grow and the world we live in changes, these strategies may begin to limit our experiences in ways that no longer serve us. If we are not conscious

"Healer Within" © *Megan Vafis 1991*

11

of what's really going on for us, we can get caught in abusive cycles, directed either at ourselves or toward others. When we begin to get in touch with the truth of our experience, and start to receive validation for that, the healer within becomes empowered. She holds both our wounded self and our free self. She holds the well-armored amazon defender who doesn't trust anybody and acts out against herself or others. She also holds the natural wild child of our innocence, who is hiding from a world that is not safe, somewhere no one can find or hurt her again. As the different parts of us begin to accept and communicate with each other, healing begins to happen.

Only by touching the pain and trusting our experiences will our pain and experiences lead us to their source and open the way for transformation. The healer within is like our own special version of the Great Mother: there is room on her lap for everybody, for all parts of ourselves, for the whole of creation. When we begin to get in touch with the healer within, the little seed of trust buried deep inside ourselves can begin to open up to the light and warmth of life's embrace again and sprout. With her there, we have an ally who has resources, tools, and powers beyond what our wounded selves can imagine. We can begin to let in new experience, new information, new options – and get some support. That tender sprout of our healing self needs a lot of sun and water. We may start to honor the wisdom of our inner experience and accept the guidance of the healer within. We may reach out and open up to the help that is given. We no longer just get lost in the jungle of weeds where our old wounds grow wild, close off the sunlight, and take all the rainwater. Little by little, we send our roots deep into the earth to an ongoing supply of water and grow a sturdy stalk that stands on its own, with leaves that store the energy of the sunlight. We become more self-sustaining. As our buds turn into blossoms, and fruits into seeds, we become more of our whole self. We flourish and falter, create and die back again into the earth, in the ever-renewing, ever-forgiving cycles of growth that are a natural part of healing. And so the healer within transforms the world – breaking the cycle of abuse and becoming part of the cycle of growth. As we compost old hurts, defenses that no longer serve us break down into fodder for new life, creating fertile ground to heal the wounds of the world. Breaking free from the cycles of abuse and reclaiming our power are very real ways that personal journeys have global effects.

As we do this amazing work, we find allies and tools such as support groups, therapy, community, and creative work. We sustain each other and ourselves, holding ropes as we journey down into the underworld and back out again. Survivors moonifest many of the problems of society, and so their teachings are urgent on the planet today. Arising from the underworld with new wisdom, survivors become healers, and often can serve as guides to others who have lost their way.

As this **We'Moon** connects us with the power of the natural cycles, it also attempts to be a resource – a communication of support, a hand outstretched so that we know we are not alone. In creating this book, we have woven the magic and support of many wimmin, both those who sent in material and those who helped in the weaving process. We are blessed by these wonderful works of art: the hard-won fruits of wimmin's healing journeys. We have been careful during this process to honor the healing experience at every stage as well as our own issues as they arose. Deep Blessings to all Survivors! May we all continue to transform our hurts, put them in the compost bin, and tend them with sun and self love. May we rage and cry, create and change. Blessed Be.

¤ *Pandora and Musawa 1994*

"The Healer Within"   ¤ *Bev Severn 1993*

How to Use This Book
Astrological Keys

Signs: The twelve signs of the zodiac (♈ Aries through ♓ Pisces) are a mandala in the sky, marking off 30° segments in the 360° circle around the Earth. Signs show major shifts in planetary energy through the cycles. The times at which planets or the Sun enter new signs are given under the date each day, as well as in the ephemeris tables (pp. 204-209).

Moon Sign: The Moon sign is written in beside the Moon phase every day. The Moon changes signs approximately every 2 ¹/₂ days, going through all twelve signs of the zodiac every 28 days (the sidereal month). The Moon sign reflects qualities of your core inner self. See "Moon Signs: Transits" (pp. 21-22).

Sun Sign: The Sun enters a new sign once a month (around the 20th or so), completing the whole circle of the zodiac in one year. Your birthday indicates your Sun sign – where the Sun was on the day you were born – and celebrates the return of the Sun to that point each year. The Sun sign describes qualities of your visible personality, your outward shining self. See "Sun Signs: Journey" (pp. 18-20).

Days of the Week: Days of the week are named in alternating languages (English, German, French, Spanish): Monday through Friday on one page; Saturday and Sunday on the facing page. Each day is associated with a planet whose symbol appears in the line above it (e.g., ☽☽☽ is for Moon: Monday, Moonday, Luna Day).

Annual Predictions: For an astrological portrait of this year for you, you might want to turn to Gretchen Lawlor's prediction for your Sun sign, even before the year begins (see p. 16). These are located in the calendar pages around the month of your birthday, on the same page where the Sun enters a new sign.

Planets: Planets are like chakras in our solar system allowing for different frequencies or types of energies to be expressed. In the calendar pages, arrows indicate planets moving into new signs (e.g., ♃→♎). Through the ages and across cultures, there has been remarkable agreement as to the qualities of energy associated with each planet (e.g., Venus=love; see chart of Planets and Goddesses, p. 28, for brief outline). In the clock of the sky, each planet has its own rhythm of orbit. An introduction to planetary cycles in our lives is given by Sandra Pastorius (p. 200). The planet shows the type and frequency of energy, and the sign it is in shows how that energy is used.

Ephemeris: Exact planetary positions are given in the ephemeris tables in

14

back, showing where each planet is in the zodiac every day at noon GMT, for those who want to synchronize their personal cycles with the ongoing flow of universal cycles.

Aspects: The little squiggles written in under the date each day show the angle of relation between different planets (in PST: Pacific Standard Time and PDT: Pacific Daylight Savings Time). It is like an astrological weather forecast for the day, indicating which energies appear to be working together easily and well and which combinations are more challenging. See "Significant Aspects" (p. 17) for a brief explanation. The following notations are also given in the aspects:

D v/c – **Moon Void of Course:** The time just before the Moon changes into a new sign is a good time to ground and center yourself – otherwise it can be a bit disorienting. The Moon is said to be Void of Course from the last significant lunar aspect (marked v/c next to that time in the aspects) until the Moon enters a new sign.

ApG/PrG – Apogee (ApG): This is the point in the orbit of a planet or the Moon that is farthest from Earth. The effects of transits at this time may be less noticeable immediately, but may appear later on. A good time to plant root crops. **Perigee (PrG)** is the point in the orbit of a planet or the Moon that is nearest to Earth. Transits with the Moon or other planets when they are PrG will be more intense. A good time to plant above-ground crops.

sR, sD – **Retrograde or Direct:** The times when a planet goes Retrograde (sR) or Direct (sD) are also marked in the daily aspects. This indicates whether the planets are moving backward or forward through the signs of the zodiac (an optical illusion, much like being on a moving train passing a slower train, which appears to be going backward). In direct motion, planetary energies are more straightforward; in retrograde, planetary energies turn back in on themselves, are more involuted.

Time Zones: To calculate for your area, see World Time Zones chart on the last page of the Introduction (p. 31).

Eclipses: Solar eclipses occur only at new Moon, lunar ones only at full Moon. The time of greatest eclipse is given, which in general is not the exact time of the conjunction or opposition. For lunar eclipses, the magnitude is also given, in decimal form (e.g., .881 magn.). It is the fraction of the moon's diameter obscured by the shadow of the Earth. For partial solar eclipses, the magnitude is also given. For total and annular solar eclipses, the duration of the eclipse, in minutes and seconds, is given. For a more detailed discussion see "Eclipses 1995" (p. 27).

How to Use the Annual Predictions

The first thing many women do with the **We'Moon** is turn to the astrological predictions for their sun sign, to see what's in store for them in the year ahead. And then of course they turn to the predictions for the signs of their loved ones. Some read them aloud in birthday ceremonies, some send copies as New Year or birthday greetings. I'm continually astounded by the feedback from women all over the world about how personally accurate these overviews are. If you don't know your sun sign, find the one whose dates encompass your birthdate.

If you are born at the beginning or the end of the dates, you need to refer to the year you were born to find out exactly which sun sign you are. Dates vary slightly each year. Read them both if you are on the cusp of two signs. If you are versed in astrology, you can combine your sun and rising sign predictions for more specific information.

I do my best to catch wisely the essence for you in 300 words or less, but the picture is more detailed. There's just not enough room for information about specific timing or about retrogrades, eclipses, asteroids, or minor configurations. And remember, this description is only based on your sun sign – it applies to everyone born in the same month! You can imagine how much more precise it could be if information about your rising sign, moon sign, and the configuration of other planets could also be included.

© Gretchen Lawlor 1994

Planetary Movements
in 1995

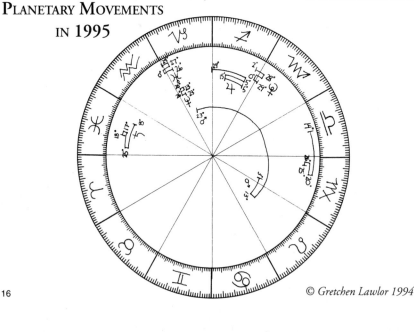

© Gretchen Lawlor 1994

WE'MOON HERBS
INTRODUCTION

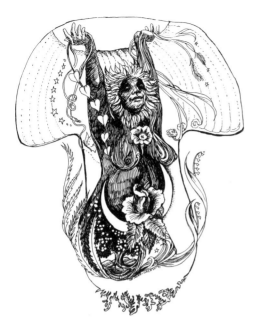

@ *Mari Jackson 1991*

Flowers gift us with sweet energies that are intensely concentrated and potent. They raise the spirits of we'moonkind, quicken our inner healing capabilities, and work simultaneously with our physical and subtle bodies.

For thousands of years the world over, we have benefited from flowers and meditated on their beauty and grace. We can return Flora's gifts by cultivating and nurturing both wild and tamed flowers in our gardens. In 1995, **We'Moon** celebrates the medicine flowers that have been our companions and supporters for millennia.*

Scientific research now connects the healing activity of flowers with flavonoids: the coloring compounds in plants that strengthen collagen tissue, blood vessels, the heart, and circulation in general. They also have anti-oxidant and anti-inflammatory effects. Long before these discoveries and explanations, our foremothers used healing flowers, fresh or dried, everyday as medicine foods in salads, soups and stews, and for teas, infusions, or tisane mixtures. They infused flowers into oils, vinegars, or alcohol for out-of-season uses; they prepared salves, lotions, and liniments. You can also dilute alcohol or vinegar-based Mother tinctures, five-, ten-, or a hundredfold, to yield flower essence tinctures which may be used homeopathically.

A simple flower can be floated in a bowl of warmed water: an offering to the senses, the soul, the goddess. As the aromatic oils diffuse through home and heart, channels open, old blockages slip away, senses are replenished and strengthened, and energies increase. Our bodies and spirits renewed, we are comforted and healed.

*Pollen-sensitive wimmin need to approach flower healing with prudence, using small amounts of flower remedies at first, then gradually increasing amounts to lessen reactivity.

© *Billie Potts 1994*   17

Sun Signs: Journey through the Year
A Story of the Gifts of Each Sign

Great Mother called Her twelve daughters together and said:

Now the time has come for you to prepare yourselves for your travel through life.

To each of you, I will give a special gift with a seed of life – so each will have a task different from the other.

Sometimes you will not have it easy on your way, and you might get dissatisfied with or jealous of each other. But you will learn to see that each of you is WHOLE, when you will have found out that all twelve of you are ONE.

And you should never forget
that I will always be   our circle of thirteen
with all of you,   is the dance
because...   of LOVE.

♈ **ARIES:** You are my first daughter – nothing yet exists, all has still to be done – so to you I give the energy of the starting Fire. Often, you will not have the time to see things growing which you have started, because there will always be something new for you to begin. Therefore, you will be quick-burning and spontaneous like a volcano, and you will have a strong will to get what you want. You will also always have your own independent way. But beware not to get impatient, irritated, or intolerant with the ones that are not like you.

♉ **TAURUS:** To you, my second daughter, I give the energy of the fixed Earth, and the ability to be sensual. You are the one who will give life, love, and substance to everything which Aries has started. You will be constructive, practical, and concrete, and you will have the patience to hold out and finish things, so that others can count on you. Don't get upset when others don't love things the way you do, and take care: your love feelings for everything you give to life can make you possessive, stubborn, and closed to changes. Don't keep your feelings inside you; learn to show them.

♊ **GEMINI:** To you, my third daughter, I give the energy of the mutable Air. You will have the ability to ask questions from all sides. You are the one who brings a mental consciousness to what is there, and from your curiosity, you will show others what they can see around them. You are open to meet anyone, and you are very social. The duality within you will make you always open to see and hear the other side of anything. On your way you will also meet indecision, restlessness, and confusion in yourself, which might confuse others and make you tend towards seeing things as all or nothing, so you will have to learn clarity.

♋ **CANCER:** You are my fourth daughter, to whom I give the energy of soft cardinal Water, with which you will be able to bring feelings to the others. You like to spread around cozy, warm, joyful, and caring energies, and you will be able to create a home for you and others wherever you are. Because you are very sensitive and therefore vulnerable, you will often protect yourself by hiding in your shell. It's important for you to learn how much you can give at one time, so you don't have to make the walls around you so hard and keep everybody far from your soft center self.

♌ **LEO:** You are my fifth daughter, and to you I give the energy of the fixed Fire, the Sun. Like the Sun, you will bring warmth, happiness, and fun. You can make everything shine with delight, and you open hearts. You will always need others around you and you will often feel in the center, but you should never make the mistake to think you are the center, because your pride can kill your innocence. Like a child you will like to play, but you should also learn that you have to lose sometimes. You love drama not only on the stage, but also in your life.

♍ **VIRGO:** To you, my sixth daughter, I give the energy of the mutable Earth. You are the last one of this first half circle which is forming the "I." So it is up to you to review and analyze all that has happened until now. You will have the tendency to check things out and criticize, but even though you will sometimes have to care for what others don't see, don't forget to leave them their space too. You will sometimes need a leader or guide, and you will be able to serve well without questioning. Your deep connection to the Earth will often make you choose nature as your teacher, and this will open you for magic, healing, and a healthy way of life. Your ability to see details and give an order to things will always help you on your way, but take care not to get stuck in them.

♎ **LIBRA:** You are my seventh daughter, and to you I give the energy of the cardinal Air. You are starting the second half of this circle, so you are the first one to come out of her own world to meet the other. You can be very charming and you have a strong sense of beauty. You have love for everybody, and with your need for justice you will always try to harmonize, to balance. Therefore, you will always need to find the balance in yourself, to find your own center point. Mostly, you will find it hard to choose, to make your own choice, because you can see the good side in everything.

♏ **SCORPIO:** To you, my eighth daughter, belongs the energy of the deep fixed Water. I give you the difficult task to experience and learn about death and rebirth. So you will be the one who can show others the impermanence of all; you show how to let go and free the way for something new. A vital force and sexual power will be available to you, because you have to deal with the regeneration of life, which will bring you often into dark, depressing, and destructive spaces. Your deepness will make you able to come to the bottom of everything, and then rise again like a colorful bird to the heights of the sky.

♐ **SAGITTARIUS:** To you, my ninth daughter, I give the energy of the mutable Fire. You will have the lightness, the optimism, and the hope to look for the truth of life – the "why" of our existence – and to find it. With your love for adventures, nothing can ever stop you from going after your goals. However, this energy can also make you restless, because once you have reached your goal you won't be satisfied until you have found the next. Your search will never be just for yourself – you have a strong need to make known what philosophical answers you have found. You will be very convinced of your own ideas, but take care not to get dogmatic or fanatic.

♑ **CAPRICORN:** You are my tenth daughter, and to you I give the energy of the starting Earth. While Sagittarius still had all the wideness in front of her to explore, you have reached the borders. You have the great wisdom that there are structures in everything. You have a strong feeling of responsibility, and you will be able to bring structures, rules, and discipline into life with others, wherever it is needed. You have a lot of endurance to go the hard and lonely ways, but take care not to get lost in your ambition. Being so strongly grounded, you are able to make high jumps and come down safely again.

♒ **AQUARIUS:** To you, my eleventh daughter, I give the energy of the fixed Air. You don't need structures anymore, you can cross the borders. You will bring the dream to the others that everything is possible; you are open to the future. This makes you free and unbounded – but for others you can sometimes be distant or superficial. At the same time, your universal mind thinks of everybody, so you will always be a good friend: playful, helpful, and gentle. You can fly very high and see everything, but you can also easily lose contact with your surroundings.

♓ **PISCES:** To you, my twelfth and last daughter, I give the energy of the mutable flowing Water. Your task is to find that all is nothing and nothing is all, which can be a painful and depressing lesson. Your compassion will help you on the way. You will be the one who dissolves everything in a total flow of feelings. You feel at home in the oceans of the subconscious, and you like to swim along on mystical waves. But you can also get very lost in the mud. You have the ability to take shape after your surroundings, so you can adapt easily, feel into others, and flow with every change. Take care, however; this passivity can also be your weak point.

Collectively written by Les Femmes de Bouichette, Rouvenac, S. France,
reprinted from **We'Moon Almanac '85.**

The Moon's passage into each of the twelve signs reflects subliminal shifts in our awareness. We may use the available energies of each sign to focus our activities and inspire our creativity.

♈ **ARIES,** The Promising Moon. Aries initiates activities and urges self-assertion. Restlessness and discontent fuel exploration, fresh approaches, and discoveries. We are quick to express feelings, attitudes, and desires. This vividly appreciative energy is nice for design and color work.

When **dark**: awaken adventure. When **full**: quests quicken.

♉ **TAURUS,** The Sensuous Moon. Appreciative Taurus energy loves the physical plane. This is a good time to beautify surroundings and acquire belongings. Intuitive touch can inspire works of art, massage, or lovemaking. Tend to bodily needs and pleasures now. Music and song are Taurean enhancements that embellish our lives.

When **dark**: truly touching. When **full**: behold the bold.

♊ **GEMINI,** The Smiling Moon. The verbal possibilities for witty exchanges expand during playful Gemini. These are good times for reading, writing, scripting, theatre, improvisation, comedy, meetings, potlucks, and parties. Restlessness may fuel short trips, explorations, family visits, and fun times.

When **dark**: catalyze concepts. When **full**: mutable solutions.

♋ **CANCER,** The Mothering Moon. Both vulnerability and strength surface with our Cancerian love for inclusive nurturance. Fertility of body and spirit feeds our inclinations towards home, family, and our places of power within. Creative folk and culinary arts may be enjoyed. Gardening and planting have fruitful results now.

When **dark**: hold your own. When **full**: fruition's feast.

♌ **LEO,** The Performing Moon. Leo generates feelings of being special. Generous warmth and vitality come easily. Romantic interludes and creative outbursts are possible. This childlike and extroverted energy enhances all aspects of theatre work, broadcasting, movement, and dance. Exhibiting, costumes, and adornments are all highlighted.

When **dark**: ardent arousal. When **full**: rave reviews.

♍ **VIRGO,** The Healing Moon. It's time for self-improvement when the Moon channels Virgo. Preciseness of intent and mental dexterity can be accessed now. Allow the attention to detail and organizational abilities of Virgo to shore up projects. Assess health care needs and dietary habits now. Crafts, repetitive designs, and collections are favorable expressions of Virgo.

When **dark**: organize priorities. When **full**: adjust attitudes.

♎ **LIBRA,** <u>The Artistic Moon</u>. Venus-ruled Libra is a mentor of the arts. Beauty, balance, harmony, cooperation, and poetic flow are her gifts. A good performing and social-gathering time. Enjoy galleries and museums. Both friendly attractions and love connections can be delightful.

When **dark**: balance bonds. When **full**: entertain allies.

♏ **SCORPIO,** <u>The Witching Moon</u>. Our natural inclinations to explore the mysteries surface during Scorpio. Masks come on or off as passions well up. Intimacy and personal disclosures may be intense, while raw honesty may be confrontive. Private space assists our deep reflection. This is a good time for intuitive arts, rituals, and divination.

When **dark**: mystical messages; When **full**: tales of power.

♐ **SAGITTARIUS,** <u>The Teaching Moon</u>. During Sagittarius free expression is energized. Opinions are valued, and tongues are swift and sure. Teaching and promotional activities come easily. Our gregariousness can feed gatherings of all kinds. Sagittarius stimulates a love of learning and movement. Exercise your freedom to travel.

When **dark**: feed beliefs. When **full**: wise aspirations.

♑ **CAPRICORN,** <u>The Building Moon</u>. We can solidify our intentions in the material world during Capricorn. Ambition, work, diligence, and duty combine with strength of will and commitment to purpose. The slow, step-by-step processes using natural materials can be applied now.

When **dark**: ambitions arise. When **full**: assume importance.

♒ **AQUARIUS,** <u>The Visionary Moon</u>. This can be an unconventional and offbeat time when unique outpourings, spontaneity, and innovation flow more easily. We can be seers of future times as our vision and insight get catalyzed in Aquarius. This is a good gathering time for brainstorming and community exchange.

When **dark**: remember the future. When **full**: revolutionary rewards.

♓ **PISCES,** <u>The Poetic Moon</u>. Our emotions and feelings are the creative elements during Pisces. Unconscious motivations and old hurts may influence our moods. Seeking solitude to recharge our inner batteries may also enhance our intuitive imagination and dreamtime. Music can heighten our spirits.

When **dark**: sensitive proximities. When **full**: empowering empathy.

LUNAR RHYTHM

The Moon has a special power for womyn: we of the Moon, we'moon! Her cycles run in our blood. She embodies the deep soul watery wiccan flow of we'moon experience. She makes the invisible visible with her light that softens rather than sharpens differences and lets other lights shine with her. We see ourselves more clearly in her light. She shows us that the whole is greater than all the different parts. We are not afraid of changes or differences – like the many faces of the Moon, we are one.

Everything that flows moves in rhythm with the Moon. She rules the water element on Earth. She pulls on the ocean's tides, the weather, female reproductive cycles, the life fluids in plants, animals, and people. She influences the underground currents in earth energy, the mood swings of mind, body, behavior, and emotion. The Moon is closer to the earth than any other heavenly body. The Earth actually has two primary relationships in the universe: one with the Moon who circles around her and one with the Sun whom she circles around. Both are equal in her eyes. The phases of the Moon reflect the dance of all three: the Moon, the Sun, and the Earth, who together weave the web of light and dark into our lives. No wonder so much of our life on Earth is intimately connected with the phases of the Moon!

The Moon has long been associated with the Triple Goddess: Maiden (Crescent), Mother (Full), and Crone (Dark Moon). What happens with the fourth phase (new/waxing/full/waning)? We'moon are beginning to reclaim the Matriarch phase (after Full Moon / Mother and before the Dark Moon / Crone). In so doing, we reinstate the fourth phase of the Goddess, and give substance to the beginning of the waning time, when the Moon (and we'moon!) are still shining their light out into the world with great power. This also frees the Crone to be in her full power in old age, at the crossroads between the worlds where her wise counsel is most needed.   ¤ *Musawa*

¤ *Megan Wilson 1992*

THE EIGHT LUNAR PHASES

As above, so below. Look into the sky and observe which phase the Moon is in. Then you will know where you are in the growth cycle of each lunar month. As we'moon heal ourselves from patriarchal violence and insanity, by observing the eternal lunar cycle we can create structure and a cohesive pattern in our lives.

1. The New **Moon** is like a SEED planted in the earth. We cannot see her but she is ready to grow, full of potential and energy for her new journey.
2. The **Crescent Moon** is the SPROUT. The seed has broken through the earth and reaches upward as she ventures from the dark moist earth she has known.
3. The **First Quarter Moon** (waxing half moon) is the GROWTH phase. Roots go deeper, the stem shoots up, and leaves form as she creates a new strong body.
4. The **Gibbous Moon** is the BUD of the plant, the pulse of life tightly wrapped, wanting to expand.
5. She opens and blossoms during the **Full Moon** phase into the FLOWER, with the desire to share her beauty with others.
6. As we go into the darkening phase of the **Disseminating Moon,** we get the FRUIT of the plant's life cycle, the fruits of wisdom and experience.
7. The **Last Quarter Moon** phase (waning half moon) is the HARVEST, when the plant gives her life so that others may continue theirs.
8. The **Balsamic Moon** phase is when the nutrients remain in the soil, the compost and mulch, to provide nourishment for the next new seed.

© *Susan Levitt*

Note: On the calendar pages, we give the exact times of the four cardinal points of the Moon phases that divide the month into four lunar weeks (in PST and GMT). Each Moon cycle begins with New Moon when the Sun and the Moon are *conjunct* (☉☌☽). Full Moon is two weeks later, in the middle of the Moon month when Sun and Moon are *in opposition* (☉☍☽). The Waxing and Waning Half Moons ("First Quarter" and "Last Quarter" Moons) occur in between, when the Sun and Moon are *square* to each other (☉□☽). Each of the eight Moon phases lasts three to four days: 1-2 days on either side of the four cardinal points, as well as the 3-4 days in between (the Crescent, Gibbous, Disseminating, and Balsamic Moon phases). This may vary for you. See what feels right in tracking the phases of your growing each Moon cycle.

❑ *Musawa 1994*

Moon Time
and Sun Cycle Correspondences

As the Moon goes around the earth in one month,
she slowly pulls a white veil of sunlight across her dark face...

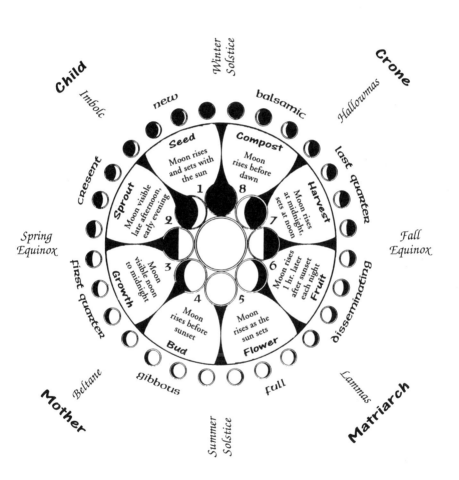

THE WHEEL OF THE YEAR: HOLY DAYS

The seasonal cycle of the year is created by the tilt of the Earth's axis as she leans towards the Sun in the north or south at different points in her annual dance around the Sun. *Solstices* are the extremes in the Sun cycle (like new and full Moon) when days and nights are either longest or shortest. At *equinoxes,* days and nights are equal (like the waxing or waning half Moons), before tipping the balance toward the light or dark side of the Sun cycle. The four *cross-quarter days* roughly mark the midpoints in between the solstices and equinoxes, giving eight seasonal "holy days" based on the natural cycles. Most traditional holidays are centered around these natural events.

If you do not find your traditional holidays in the **We'Moon**, do not be upset. Just look for the nearest lunar or solar cycle turning point, and it is bound to be very close. Only the names, dates, and specific events of the holidays have changed through the ages according to the prevailing culture. There are still some cultures today (such as Hindu, Jewish, Muslim, and Buddhist) that honor the lunar cycles by celebrating many holidays on new and full Moons. At the root of all people's cultures – if you dig far enough – is a reverence for Mother Earth and a celebration of the natural cycles throughout the seasons of Earth's passage in relation to her closest relatives in the universe.

Monica Sjöö 1992

We use the fixed dates from the Gregorian calendar for the cross-quarter days, although traditionally they are lunar holidays. Beltane (May Day) and Lammas (Harvest Moon) are Full Moon festivals at which fertile, abundant creative energy is celebrated – the time of ovulation and conception in we'moon cycles. Samhain (Hallowmas) and Imbolc (Candlemas) are traditionally Dark Moon festivals, when death and rebirth, the crone, and the underworld journey are celebrated – the time in tribal cultures when we'moon bleed together. The cross-quarter days are fire festivals celebrating the height of each season, when the subtle shifts in energy, initiated as the balance points at Solstice and Equinox, begin to be visible in nature. For example, the increasing amount of daylight that is accelerating around Spring Equinox begins to be noticeable by May Day.   □ *Musawa*

ECLIPSES 1995

A solar eclipse is a conjunction of the Sun and the Moon. This occurs only at the time of the new Moon. A solar eclipse can be either partial, total, or annular. An annular eclipse occurs when the Moon is at apogee and the surface of the Moon is not large enough to completely block out the Sun. As a result, the Sun leaves a light ring around the Moon.

A lunar eclipse is an opposition of the Sun and the Moon. This occurs only during the time of the full Moon. A lunar eclipse only occurs 14 days before or after a solar eclipse. Total, partial, and appulse eclipses are the forms of lunar eclipse. During an appulse eclipse, the body of the Moon only receives the light of the Sun from one side of the Earth. This produces a darkening of the Moon's surface.

Since ancient times, astrologers have used the eclipse as a form of prediction and delineation of events. Eclipses bring us in touch with our dark side: fears, wild woman selves, emotional patterns, animal natures. During the time of the eclipse a crack in ordinary reality appears. We can use this information to create a window for change, on any level, and specifically to evolve our emotional consciousness.

To determine the effect of an eclipse, check your natal chart. In what house does the eclipse fall? This will determine the specific emphasis of the eclipse (e.g., first house – body, seventh house – relationships, etc.). If the eclipse is in opposition or conjunction to any planets the emphasis becomes a crisis (i.e., a requirement for us to devote more time and attention to whatever area of our life the eclipse emphasizes). The more personal the planets, the stronger the influence.   © *Mari Susan Selby 1993*

1995 eclipses occur April 5, April 29, October 8, and October 23.

PLANETS

<u>Personal Planets</u> are the ones closest to the Earth.

Mercury ☿ : communication, conscious thought, inventiveness

Venus ♀ : relationship, love, sense of beauty and sensuality, empathy

Mars ♂ : will to act, initiative, ambition

<u>Asteroids</u> are found between Mars and Jupiter. They bridge the personal and the social planets. They reflect the rebirth of the Goddess, and the awakening of feminine-defined energy centers in the human consciousness. See "Why Asteroids?" (p. 202).

<u>Social Planets</u> are in between the personal planets and the outer planets.

Jupiter ♃ : expansion, opportunities, leadership

Saturn ♄ : limits, structure, discipline

<u>Chiron</u> ⚷ is situated between Saturn and Uranus and bridges the social and transpersonal planets. Chiron represents the wounded healer, the core wound that leads us to our path of service. See "Chiron" (p. 30).

<u>Transpersonal Planets</u> are the outer planets. They are slow-moving and influence generational issues.

Uranus ♅ : revolutionary change, cosmic consciousness

Neptune ♆ : spiritual awakening, cosmic love, all one

Pluto ♇ : death and rebirth, purification, takes us to the depths where total change is possible

*In the matriarchal zodiac, the planets are named after goddesses.
Excerpted from *Matriarchal Zodiac* © *Blue Moonfire 1985*

GODDESSES*

Metis: counsel, wisdom
Aphrodite: grace and love
Dione: sexuality, growth, struggle

Themis: time, justice, prophecy
Rhea: natural order and peace

Urania: heaven and earth
Tethys: the seas
Persephone: death in life, life in death

ASPECTS

Aspects show the angle between planets in the 360° circle of the sky. This relationship informs how the planets, and the signs in which they are, influence each other. The **We'Moon** lists only the major aspects:

☌ CONJUNCTION (planets are 0-5° apart)
  linked together, energy of aspected planets is mutually enhancing

⚹ SEXTILE (planets are 60° apart)
  cooperative, energies of this aspect blend well

☐ SQUARE (planets are 90° apart)
  challenging, energies of the aspect are different from each other

△ TRINE (planets are 120° apart)
  harmonizing, energies of this aspect are in the same element

☍ OPPOSITION (planets are 180° apart)
  polarizing or complementing, energies are diametrically opposite

Surviving Pluto in Scorpio

Pluto is one of the slower-moving, collective or transcendent planets, spending many years in one Sign. Since 1984, Pluto has been transiting through the Sign it rules: Scorpio. Both Pluto and Scorpio represent the power of transformation, the process of elimination, and the underworld of things hidden or secret. They symbolize the alchemical change from one state of Life to another, and teach the process of letting go. Transformation occurs seasonally as the Earth grows close to and then away from the Sun. During Autumn when the Sun is in Scorpio, the fullness of Summer's growth dies away. Symbolically, we experience transformation in our personal lives when we come to a crisis point, and push through our old forms and ways, letting go to the next phase of our evolution.

As Pluto's journey through Scorpio comes to a close in 1995, our deepest urgings and motivations are surfacing. Pluto has exposed the underworld of our collective psyche during these last eleven years, and opened up our memories of wounding, especially in the areas of sexuality, for Scorpio rules sexual intimacy and taboos. The brew of the underworld has been stirred, as the silence about sexual and substance abuses has been broken and the underground recovery movement swells. The AIDS virus has passed from person to person bringing about havoc and fear between us, yet it is catalyzing more sexual honesty, and awareness about death with dignity and compassion. Abortion and women's rights are still in dispute, and the ugly realities of rape as a tactic of war and genocide loom in some parts of the world. With no more places to hide, as the patriarchy dissolves, our fears are emerging into full consciousness, sometimes violently. We are all in a healing crisis together.

While our depths are being purged and cleansed, our vulnerabilities expose us to the divine Feminine residing within. Her abiding wisdom affirms life, and teaches through love. Her reemergence is a source of profound healing, from which we all may be nourished. Through our acts of prayer and goodwill, we tap Her wellspring, and our surviving becomes our thriving.

As Pluto moves into fiery Sagittarius, the whole meaning of power is being transformed. We can experience rising, like the Phoenix, from our own ashes. The potency of release can be both painful and ecstatic, and fuel our creative capacities. Our challenge is to be redeemed by the dark, reclaim our inner territory, make a fearless commitment to the sacred in all, and bring joy into the heart of the human family.

The following dates show the movement of Pluto in 1995: Jan. 1-16 (Scorpio), Jan. 17-Apr. 22 (Sagittarius), Apr. 23-Nov. 10, (Scorpio retrograde), Nov. 11-Jan. 26, 2008 (Sagittarius).

© *Sandra Pastorius 1994*

CHIRON: THE WOUNDED HEALER

In November of 1977 a small planetary body was discovered in the solar system orbiting between Saturn and Uranus. It was subsequently named Chiron, after the mythological centaur who was half-horse and half-human.

Chiron was teacher, prophet, physician, and musician. He was a healer who taught the medicinal use of plants, surgery, and the laying on of hands. When Chiron was accidentally wounded in the knee by a poisoned arrow, for all his healing knowledge, he was unable to cure himself.

Archetypally, Chiron represents the quintessential shamanic healer. What distinguishes a shaman from any other kind of healer is that the shaman is always wounded first; it is the wound, in its sacred aspect, that serves as the initiation journey.

When Chiron is an active archetype in our lives, we experience a physical, psychological, or spiritual crisis which engenders great suffering. We descend into the underworld of the unconscious where we meet the shadow demons, face death, and develop a communication with the world of unseen spirits and guides. As we begin to learn the secret ways of Nature, our psychic channels are opened; we discover our special talents in our role of helping others. This experience of personal crisis, followed by a deepening of self-mastery and healing ability, is the critical act through which we can access our divine nature and heed the call for service to the community and to the planet.

The holistic health movement emerged in the year of Chiron's discovery. In particular, there emerged many support groups (for survivors of alcohol and

drug abuse, eating disorders, incest, and other forms of abuse) where "wounded healers" were helping to pull their sisters and brothers through the dark passageway to healing and wholeness.

In the astrological birthchart, Chiron speaks to the nature of our essential wound, and how this wound becomes our central life challenge through which we fulfill our destiny. Chiron's way of wisdom and healing involves connecting to the numinous world and embracing the sacred dimension of our suffering as a path of service to others.

© Demetra George 1994

"Otter Medicine Woman"
© Vicki Ledray Grabicki 1990

WORLD TIME ZONES

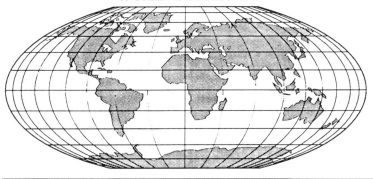

ID LW	NT BT	CA HT	YST	PST	MST	CST	EST	AST	BST	AT	WAT	GMT	CET	EET	BT	USSR Z3	USSR Z4	USSR Z5	SST	CCT	JST	GST	USSR Z10	ID LE
-12	-11	-10	-9	-8	-7	-6	-5	4	-3	-2	-1	0	+1	+2	+3	+4	+5	+6	+7	+8	+9	+10	+11	+12
-4	-3	-2	-1	0	+1	+2	+3	+4	+5	+6	+7	+8	+9	+10	+11	+12	+13	+14	+15	+16	+17	+18	+19	+20

STANDARD TIME ZONES FROM WEST TO EAST CALCULATED FROM PST AS ZERO POINT:

IDLW:	International Date Line West	-4
NT/BT:	Nome Time/Bering Time	-3
CA/HT:	Central Alaska & Hawaiian Time	-2
YST:	Yukon Standard Time	-1
PST:	Pacific Standard Time	0
MST:	Mountain Standard Time	+1
CST:	Central Standard Time	+2
EST:	Eastern Standard Time	+3
AST:	Atlantic Standard Time	+4
NFT:	Newfoundland Time	+4 1/2
BST:	Brazil Standard Time	+5
AT:	Azores Time	+6
WAT:	West African Time	+7
GMT:	Greenwich Mean Time	+8
WET:	Western European Time (England)	+8
CET:	Central European Time	+9
EET:	Eastern European Time	+10
BT:	Bagdhad Time	+11
IT:	Iran Time	+11 1/2
USSR	Zone 3	+12
USSR	Zone 4	+13
IST:	Indian Standard Time	+13 1/2
USSR	Zone 5	+14
NST:	North Sumatra Time	+14 1/2
SST:	South Sumatra Time & USSR Zone 6	+15
JT:	Java Time	+15 1/2
CCT:	China Coast Time	+16
MT:	Moluccas Time	+16 1/2
JST:	Japanese Standard Time	+17
SAST:	South Australian Standard Time	+17 1/2
GST:	Guam Standard Time	+18
USSR	Zone 10	+19
IDLE:	International Date Line East	+20

HOW TO CALCULATE TIME ZONE CORRECTIONS FOR YOUR AREA:

ADD if you are **East** of PST (Pacific Standard Time), **SUBTRACT** if you are **West** of PST on this map (see right-hand column of chart above).

All times in this calendar are calculated from the West Coast of North America where it is made. Pacific Standard Time (PST/ Zone 8) is Zero Point for this calendar except during Daylight Savings Time (April 3-October 30, 1994, during which times are given for PDT/ Zone 7). If your time zone does not use Daylight Savings Time, add one hour to the standard correction during this time. Time corrections for GMT are also given for major turning points in the Moon and Sun Cycles. At the bottom of each page EST/EDT (Eastern Standard or Daylight Time) and GMT (Greenwich Mean Time) times are also given. For all other time zones, calculate your time zone correction(s) from this map and write it on the inside cover for easy reference.

Rhea
Kali
Isis
Diana
Anu

Rhiannon
Brigid
Cerridwen
Cailleach

¤ Monica Sjöö 1983

Celebrating the Goddess

For the first 30,000 years of human existence, the Earth was celebrated and worshipped as female. All over the planet different peoples created images of the Great Mother, the Almighty Goddess in her many aspects. The mysteries of menstruation, pregnancy, and childbirth were honored and celebrated along with the abundance of the Earth and the changing of the seasons. Women were often esteemed members of society, and were the creative force in the development of agriculture, animal domestication, cooking, tools, fire use, ceramics, food storage, weaving, religion, ritual, calendars, language, writing, and more. Over a several-thousand-year period, nomadic groups of war-oriented, male-dominated people destroyed and oppressed these peaceful civilizations and instituted God the Father as Supreme Being. Despite the continuing destructive grip of patriarchy upon the land, people today are discovering and reclaiming the sacred mysteries of the Goddess, raising her back to prominence in our lives. To celebrate and recreate the Goddess today is a powerful and balancing act of personal and planetary healing.

© 1989 Marcy Marchello

0. SOLSTICE / FULL MOON

The Healing*

*See back cover art.

It came in winter,
when ice began melting into liquid
flowing pure and clean
through hollow, sunken veins -
nourishing her body,
feeding roots so long in thirst.
In the darkness of the underworld
of sorrow,
of gloom,
of longing to find the sun,
the root was tapped
and a shoot sent slowly upward,
penetrating crusts of grit and stone.
To the light of day
a single blade appeared,
delicately balanced
between the binding of the earth
and the urging of the mother root.
When the path was clearly open,
she made her way -
ascending with a careful speed,
climbing with the weight of dying anguish,
to probe the truthfulness of dawn,
to test the honor of the twilight sky.
She rose.
Silently rose.
The healing began in winter.   © *Nancy Bright 1986*

ħħħ

♊   ◯   Saturday
              17

December, 1994

☉□♇   5:20 pm
☉☍☽   6:18 pm
☽☍♅   11:24 pm   v/c

◯◯◯   Full Moon in ♊ Gemini 6:18 pm PST
                                                          2:18 GMT

♊   ◯   Sunday
♋   ◐   18

☽→♋   2:26 am
☽⚹♂   4:55 am
☽△♄   4:21 pm
♅→♑   10:27 pm

December

Healing blessings for this coming year.
Happy Solstice! — We'Moon Matrix

ⅅⅅⅅ

♋ Monday
19

☽△♀	5:02 am
☿△♂	9:40 pm
☽☍♆	10:00 pm

♂♂♂

♋
♌ Tuesday
20

☽☍♅	3:13 am	
☽△♇	11:34 am	v/c
☽→♌	1:14 pm	
☽△♃	6:01 pm	

☿☿☿

♌ Wednesday
21

| ☉→♑ | 6:24 pm |
| ☽□♀ | 6:41 pm |

Solstice

♑

♃♃♃

Sun in Capricorn 6:24 pm PST
2:24 GMT

♌
♍ Thursday
22

| ☽□♇ | 8:35 pm | v/c |
| ☽→♍ | 10:02 pm | |

♀♀♀

♍ Friday
23

☉△☽	12:23 am
☽♂♂	1:43 am
☽□♃	3:34 am
☽△♅	11:22 am
☽☍♄	11:36 am
☿⚹♄	1:23 pm
☉△♂	7:24 pm

All aspects in Pacific Standard Time; add 3 hours for EST; add 8 hours for GMT

Year at a glance for CAPRICORN ♑ (Dec. 21–Jan. 19)

In 1994 an unusual pileup of planets in Capricorn brought unsettled, unusual circumstances into your life. There were changes in home, in profession, new interests, new horizons. It was not a time to commit to long-range plans, but to experiment and keep your options open. This was challenging for Capricorns, who prefer to work in an orderly manner towards clear goals.

By 1995 all the planets but Neptune have moved on to other signs. Uranus touches Aquarius from April through June, then retrogrades for a last swipe at Capricorn until January 2, 1996. Don't expect life to return to the way things were before everything hit Capricorn. Neptune, symbolic of your impressionability and imagination, is still influential. Your dreams are vivid and haunting; you hunger for idealistic or utopian involvements. You are impressionable and vaguely discontented, and you are a new person but don't yet know what to do with yourself.

Saturn continues to move through Pisces and your solar 3rd house. Saturn's 1995 challenge to Capricorn is to improve communication skills, particularly with neighbors and siblings. Saturn in Pisces brought gloomy moods in 1994; now Jupiter helps through compassion and a more philosophical attitude regarding difficult communications. Greater understanding comes through spiritual or metaphysical interests. You will meet someone who has important things to teach you. This person will help you to discover and heal forgotten or hidden parts of you. With their encouragement you can free yourself of old guilt or regret.

Chiron hovers around your solar 10th house for all of 1995, bringing a cycle of withdrawal, introversion, and reflection, then returning you to your professional or public life. By doing your own inner healing work you become a more powerful healing force in the world. © *Gretchen Lawlor 1994*

♍ Saturday
24

☽⚹♀ 5:55 am
☽△♆ 2:46 pm
☽△♅ 7:44 pm

♍ Sunday
♎ **25**

☽⚹♇ 3:14 am v/c
☽→♎ 4:28 am
☽⚹♃ 10:36 am
☉□☽ 11:07 am

"Gathering Strength"
◻ *Debby Earthdaughter 1993*

Waning Half Moon in ♎ Libra 11:07 am PST, 19:07 GMT

Stone by Stone

Stone by stone
a fortress built
to protect a child
becomes a prison
to the woman.

With thick walls
safety is assured,
isolation is complete,
so is the cold.

After storms,
winters and time,
growing things creep
in cranny and crevice.

Stone by broken stone
ruins are open places.

© Ila Suzanne 1986

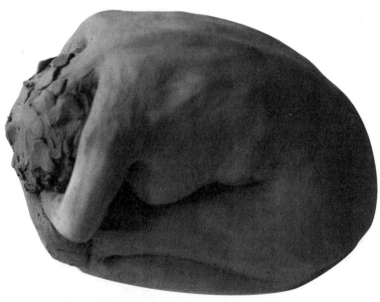

Stoney Feelings ◻ Carole Shaw 1993

Don't Look at Me ◻ Carole Shaw 1993

I. CHAOS / COPING MOON

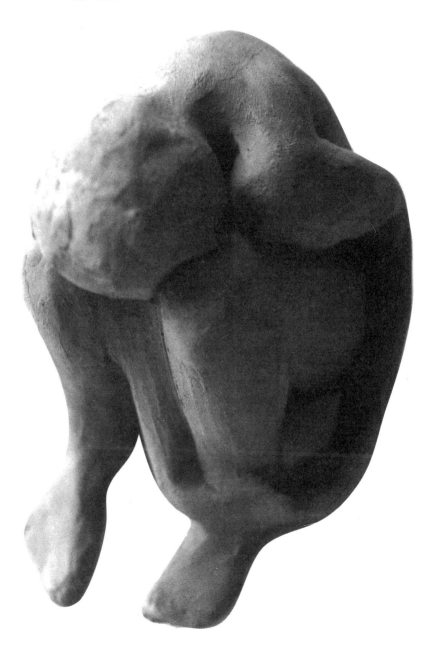

Don't Touch Me   ¤ *Carole Shaw 1993*

Dezember

♌♌♌

♎ ## Montag
26

☽□♀ 12:18 am
☽□♇ 7:24 pm

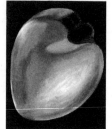

"Detached Heart"
¤ Carole Shaw 1993

♂♂♂

♎
♏ ## Dienstag
27

☽□♅ 12:12 am   v/c
☽→♏ 8:18 am
☽✶♂ 12:24 pm
☉✶☽ 6:34 pm
☽△♄ 9:10 pm

☿☿☿

♏ ## Mittwoch
28

☽✶♅ 9:31 am
☽♂♀ 7:37 pm
☽✶♇ 9:31 pm

♃♃♃

♏
♐ ## Donnerstag
29

☽✶♅ 2:11 am
☽♂♇ 8:53 am   v/c
☽→♐ 9:46 am
☉✶♄ 10:18 am
☽□♂ 1:56 pm
☽♂♃ 4:47 pm
☽□♄ 10:27 pm   v/c

♀♀♀

♐ ## Freitag
30

♀✶♇ 4:23 am
☽PrG 3:16 pm

It was for this
    I incubated in the mud,
slowly basting
    in generations of pain,
until the frozen heart
    agreed to beat again.

excerpt ¤ Sherri Rose-Walker 1991

© *Sierra Lonepine Briano 1991*

Broken Hearted Butch Madonna in a Dress

ħħħ

♐
♑

Samstag
31

☽→♑   9:58 am
☽△♂   2:13 pm
☽⚹ħ   10:51 pm

☉☉☉

♑   ●

Sonntag
1

Januar, 1995

☉♂☽   2:57 am
☽♂♅   10:17 pm
☽♂♆   10:31 pm

New Moon in ♑ Capricorn 2:57 am PST, 10:57 GMT

janvier

"Migraine Again"
¤ *Peni Hall 1989*

♑
♒ **lundi**
2

☿☌♆	12:26 am
☽⚹♀	2:44 am
☽☌♅	3:21 am
☽⚹♇	9:58 am v/c
☽→♒	10:40 am
♀⚹♅	12:51 pm
♂sR	1:14 pm
☽⚹♃	7:14 pm

♂♂♂

♒ **mardi**
3

♀⚹⚷	9:17 am
☿☌♅	9:32 pm

☿☿☿

♒
♓ **mercredi**
4

☿△⚷	8:23 am
☽□♀	9:06 am
☽□♇	1:12 pm v/c
☽→♓	1:50 pm
☽☍♂	6:30 pm
☽□♃	11:47 pm

♃♃♃

♓ **juedi**
5

☽☌♄	4:48 am
☿⚹♀	5:14 pm
☉⚹☽	5:18 pm

♀♀♀

♓
♈ **vendredi**
6

☽⚹♆	7:18 am		
☿⚹♇	9:49 am		
☽⚹♅	1:01 pm		
☿→♒	2:18 pm		
☽△♀	8:21 pm		
☽△♇	8:25 pm v/c	♀☌♇	9:07 pm
☽→♈	8:57 pm	☽⚹☿	9:56 pm

All aspects in Pacific Standard Time; add 3 hours for EST; add 8 hours for GMT

These are my Selves
that allowed me
to survive.

These are the Voices
that have carried me,
though in chaos
to where i stand now.

To my 18+ Alters,
who through 'Altering'
Saved my Life.

© Draak 1992

♄♄♄

♈ samedi
7

♀→♐ 4:08 am
☽△♃ 8:35 am

☉☉☉

♈ dimanche
8

☉□☽ 7:47 am
☽□♆ 5:41 pm
☽□♅ 11:52 pm   v/c

---

enero

♈
♉ lunes
9

☽→♉	7:59 am
☽△♂	12:44 pm
♀□♂	1:29 pm
☽□☿	6:03 pm

© *Red Raven 1993*

♉ martes
10

☽⚹♄	1:51 am
⚷sR	8:27 am
☿⚹♃	9:17 pm

♉
♊ miercoles
11

☉△☽	2:03 am
☽△♆	6:39 am
☽△♅	1:03 pm
☽ApG	2:10 pm
☽☍♇	8:41 pm	v/c
☽→♊	8:58 pm

♊ jueves
12

☽□♂	1:12 am
☽☍♀	7:20 am
☽☍♃	11:14 am
☽□♄	3:23 pm
☽△☿	4:02 pm	v/c

♊ viernes
13

| ☉☌♆ | 9:07 am |
| ♆ApG | 11:20 am |

All aspects in Pacific Standard Time; add 3 hours for EST; add 8 hours for GMT

Sweet music soothes
Like cinema
The coffee's bite vicious
Fingers deep in donut
Flesh
Chocolate cream drips
Falling drugs of daylight
In this place again
To think of death
I mask pain with sugar
All that is sweet
In my life
To sit here ordinary
Among shoppers
Is to be held

© *Berta Freistadt 1991*

Swimming in a Whirl of Emotions
© *Genece Klein 1990*

♊
♋ 🌙 sabado
14

☽→♋   9:21 am
☽⚹♂   12:46 pm
♀♂♃   1:52 pm

♋ 🌙 domingo
15

☽△♄   3:42 am

January

DDD

 *Megan Wilson 1993*

♋
♌

Monday
16

♅△⚷	5:39 am
☽☍♆	6:32 am
☉☍☽	12:27 pm
☽☍♅	12:45 pm
♀□♄	1:19 pm
☉△⚷	3:38 pm
☉♂♅	4:23 pm

☽△♇	7:37 pm v/c
☽→♌	7:37 pm

Full Moon in ♋ Cancer 12:27 pm PST, 20:27 GMT

_____ ♂♂♂ _____

♌ ## Tuesday
17

♇→♐	2:11 am
☽△♃	10:39 am
♅ApG	11:19 am
☽△♀	3:39 pm

_____ ☿☿☿ _____

♌ ## Wednesday
18

☽☍☿	2:48 am v/c

_____ ♃♃♃ _____

♌
♍

Thursday
19

☽→♍	3:40 am
☽□♇	3:46 am
☽♂♂	5:12 am
☽□♃	6:56 pm
☽☍♄	9:34 pm

_____ ♀♀♀ _____

♍ ## Friday
20

Sun in Aquarius 5:01 am PST, 13:01 GMT

☽□♀	3:48 am
☉→♒	5:01 am
☉✶♇	6:54am
☽△♆	10:00 pm

_____

All aspects in Pacific Standard Time; add 3 hours for EST; add 8 hours for GMT

Year at a glance for AQUARIUS ♒ (Jan. 20–Feb. 17)

Uranus begins a seven-year transit of your sign on March 1, 1995. Despite a short retrograde into Capricorn, significant change is set in motion. Uranus represents our most unconventional self. As it transits through Aquarius, people in general will be more individualistic. And for you Aquarians, who often go that extra mile to be different, your unconventional side will really be empowered. You need a purpose or cause, or you could waste your time being destructive and rebellious. Your willingness to experiment is a great inspiration to those around you.

For several years, as Uranus approached Aquarius, you have been hungering for change, but have not been able to act. Now is the time. Old dreams and ideals don't seem important any more. You feel restless and impatient; you want to relate to life in a radically different way – right now. If you resist change, circumstances will force it upon you.

Aquarians are attracted to humanitarian or political organizations. Right now, not only Uranus, but also Jupiter and Pluto are affecting those involvements. You align yourself with radical movements and intense interactions; casual friendships have no place in your present program. You will be plunged into an entirely new social circle in your dedicated pursuit of these interests. Your friendships have a purpose in your individual development at this time; they help you confront new dimensions of yourself.

Saturn continues its transit through your 2nd house, challenging you to be resourceful, to make do with less. You may start a new business from scratch or acquire practical training that will become a means of income in the future. Even with this focus on your material circumstances, spiritual values will dominate your life and color your decisions.

© Gretchen Lawlor 1994

♄♄♄

♍ ♎

Saturday 21

☽△♅ 3:59 am v/c
☽→♎ 9:55 am
☽✶♇ 10:06 am
☉△☽ 12:16 pm

☉☉☉

♎

Sunday 22

☽✶♃ 1:25 am
♂□♇ 4:25 am
☽✶♀ 1:51 pm
℞♂→♌ 3:49 pm
☽△☿ 10:09 pm

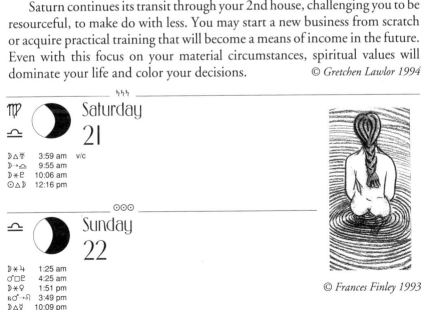

© Frances Finley 1993

Januar

♎︎
♏︎ ## Montag
23

☽□♆	3:08 am	
☽□♅	9:01 am	
☽⚹♂	2:07 pm	v/c
☽→♏︎	2:33 pm	
☉□☽	8:59 pm	

Waning Half Moon in ♏︎ Scorpio 8:59 pm PST
4:59 GMT

♏︎   ## Dienstag
24

☽△♄	8:12 am

♏︎
♐︎ ## Mittwoch
25

☽□♉	2:51 am	
☽⚹♆	6:41 am	
☽⚹♅	12:28 pm	
☽□♂	4:12 pm	v/c
☿sR	5:10 pm	
☽→♐︎	5:38 pm	
☽☌♇	5:58 pm	

♐︎ ## Donnerstag
26

☉⚹☽	3:45 am
☽☌♃	9:29 am
☽□♄	11:09 am

♐︎
♑︎ ## Freitag
27

☽☌♀	4:14 am	
☽⚹♉	4:41 am	
☿⚹♀	9:05 am	
☽PrG	3:35 pm	
☽△♂	5:01 pm	v/c
☽→♑︎	7:27 pm	

All aspects in Pacific Standard Time; add 3 hours for EST; add 8 hours for GMT

© Melissa Harris 1992

Borage Flowers *Borago officinalis*

The intense bright blue stars that are borage flowers lift our spirits in the dark of the year. They support, restore, and stimulate our adrenals, and provide minerals and flavonoids for healing the skin, lungs, and heart, and for enhancing our coping capabilities.

During the growing season, the flowers make delicious fairy-salad food and stress-relieving teas. Keep picking the flowers to encourage more blooms; dry on screens away from light and heat to provide a store for tea. Tincture the flowers in season and prepare syrups, lotions, and salves for use during winter stress, sadness, or depression.   © *Billie Potts 1994*

_____ ♄♄♄ _____

♑ Samstag
28

☽⚹♄   1:08 pm

_____ ☉☉☉ _____

♑ Sonntag
♒ 29

☽☌♆   10:30 am
☽☌♅   4:22 pm   v/c
☽→♒   9:04 pm
☽⚹♇   9:33 pm

Ancient Stillness

Today I can do no more, every cell imbued
with fierce desire for the kindness of quiet
and the roomy queendom of the heart.
The window must be shut, cacophony held at bay
while I repair my raveled senses.
The miracle of blood demands this, reminding me,
immeshed in the white heat of accomplishment,
of ancient stillness in the leafy glade, solitude and the moon.
Within the silence, flowing around me like silken robes,
I muse, measure and meditate,
pausing often for the bitter, holy tide of memory to rise up
washing me clean of intention.
Only so cleansed do I hear the humming of the winged folk,
canticles of still, secret music that heals.

¤ Sherri Rose-Walker 1991

II. SOLITUDE / SILENCE MOON

Menses Introspection
¤ *Tamara Thiebaux 1991*

janvier

𝓓𝓓𝓓

≈

lundi
30

☉✶♃	3:10 am
☽✶♃	2:06 pm
☉☌☽	2:49 pm

Lunar Imbolc
New Moon in ≈ Aquarius 2:49 pm PST, 22:49 GMT

♂♂♂

≈

mardi
31

☽☌♉	4:17 am
♂☓♅	9:45 am
☽✶♀	4:43 pm
☽☍♂	7:07 pm	v/c
♀□♂	9:17 pm

☿☿☿

≈
♓

mercredi
1

fevrier

☽→♓	12:06 am
☽□♇	12:40 am
♀△♂	3:53 pm
☽□♃	6:38 pm
☽☌♄	7:52 pm

♃♃♃

♓

juedi
2

Imbolc/Candlemas

☽✶♆	6:45 pm

♀♀♀

♓
♈

vendredi
3

☽✶♅	1:26 am
☽□♀	3:22 am	v/c
☽→♈	6:13 am
☽△♇	6:54 am
☉☌♉	3:01 pm

All aspects in Pacific Standard Time; add 3 hours for EST; add 8 hours for GMT

Mask for Imbolc

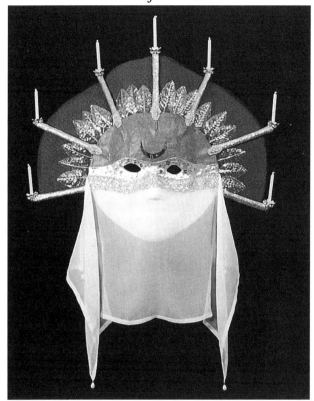

© Sheila Broun 1992

Candlemas

Candlemas or St. Brigit's Day is one of the four Celtic fire festivals which fall on the cross-quarter days, six weeks between the solstices and equinoxes. Candlemas is a time when the light of rebirth grows stronger; it is a time for retreat and rekindling of the inner fire. Brigit is the triple goddess of the flame.

Her fire was carried from the land of Brigantia on the British Isles to Kildare, not far from Dublin in Ireland. The Daughters of the Flame, nine sacred Virgins who could be looked on by no man, tended her fire; later it was tended by the Christian sisters when she became Saint Brigit (or Bridget or Brigid). Brigit's fires are the fires of purification and healing.

Candlemas is the time of the feast of poets, of the nine muses. It is a time in Wicca when priestesses are initiated into the coven. It can be a time when women dedicate themselves to the Goddess.

© Marcia Starck 1993, printed and excerpted from <u>Women's Medicine Ways: Cross-Cultural Rites of Passage</u> with permission from The Crossing Press.

Imbolc

If not for the peace
of Sunday night
in the long and delicate pause
of traffic,
this two lane road
listening

as dog curls
in his lame growl of sleep,
as the path
of an unmentioned skunk
widens, as rats shift
in shimmering bamboo,
as black cat
flexes his tail, delighted
in this glistening rain

and everything I wish for
remains silent
while I count its pulse

as neighbors turn
in their bright carriage of sleep,
the mint of contentment
on every tongue,
as daughters collapse
in the fury of their dreams, exhaling
when they reach the turnstile

as their breath pierces
one dark moon
in the heavy quiet
of predators, night wise
and slow

as coyote abandons
Saturday's deer,
as owl has her fill
of silvery rabbit,
as water slips
along the canyon rockface
like black lace
and chills the vacant night

Persephone tugs
a honeysuckle root
and waits
to be born

□ *Marcia Cohee 1993*

Sleep

© Durga Bernhard 1993

♄♄♄

♈

samedi

4

☽△♃ 2:46 am
☽✶☿ 8:22 am
☉✶☽ 11:46 am
♀→♑ 12:13 am

☉☉☉

♈
♉

dimanche

5

☽□♆ 4:05 am
☽△♂ 7:10 am
☿PrG 11:00 am
☽□♅ 11:20 am v/c
☽→♉ 4:10 pm
☽△♀ 7:01 pm

febrero

ᴅᴅᴅ

♉ lunes
6

☿✶♃ 11:56 am
☽□☿ 2:23 pm
☽✶♄ 3:42 pm

♂♂♂

♉ martes
7

☉□☽ 4:55 am
☽△♆ 4:30 pm
☽□♂ 5:34 pm

Waxing Half Moon in ♉ Taurus 4:55 am PST, 12:55 GMT

☿☿☿

♉
♊ miercoles
8

☽△♅ 12:05 am v/c
☽→♊ 4:45 am
☽☌♇ 5:38 am
☽ApG 10:07 am
☽△☿ 10:28 pm

♃♃♃

♊ jueves
9

☽☌♃ 4:18 am
☽□♄ 5:13 am
☉△☽ 11:29 pm

♀♀♀

♊
♋ viernes
10

☽✶♂ 4:24 am v/c
☽→♋ 5:18 am

All aspects in Pacific Standard Time; add 3 hours for EST; add 8 hours for GMT

© *Leslie Foxfire Stager 1992*

Quiet me, Holy One.

Gather the loose frayed ends
gently together.
Prune from me the stragglers
which steal my potency.
Wipe away the desires
which cloud my vision.

Bathe me
in the water of our intimacy.
Dry me
in the wind of trusting vulnerability.
Cradle me
in the silent stillness
of our secret place.

© *Vicki Blake 1993*

ᚻᚻᚻ

♋ sabado
11

♂PrG   6:20 am
☽☍♀   8:35 am
☽△♄   5:37 pm
☉☍♂   6:32 pm

◎◎◎

♋ domingo
12

☽☍♆   4:26 pm
☽☍♅   11:43 pm   v/c

February

ⅅⅅⅅ

♋
♌

Monday
13

☽→♌ 3:32 am
☽△♇ 4:29 am
☽☍☿ 2:42 pm

© Draak 1993

♂♂♂

♌

Tuesday
14

☽△♃ 2:28 am
☽♂♂ 7:49 pm

☿☿☿

♌
♍

Wednesday
15

☉☍☽ 4:16 am v/c
☽→♍ 10:53 am
☽□♇ 11:49 am
♀⚹♄ 7:33 pm
☿sD 9:01 pm

♃♃♃   Full Moon in ♌ Leo 4:16 am PST, 12:16 GMT

♍

Thursday
16

☽□♃ 9:18 am
☽☍♄ 9:56 am
☽△♀ 11:08 am

♀♀♀

♍
♎

Friday
17

☽△♆ 6:04 am
☽△♅ 12:55 am v/c
☽→♎ 4:01 am
☽⚹♇ 4:58 pm

Year at a glance for PISCES ♓ (Feb. 18–Mar. 19)

There's a powerful influence around Pisces this year: Pluto conjunct your solar midheaven. You've experienced career dissatisfaction or disruption of your public image in the last two to three years. Is your work meaningful? Does it engage you deeply? You may leave your work on a matter of principle. Some deep part of you wants change and will unconsciously find the circumstances that release you. Your ambitions shift to research, psychology, sexual or even taboo areas, in your field.

Your relationship with a parent is undergoing a transformation. Even if the parent died years ago, it's time for you to clear residual guilt, anger, or resentment. This clearing will also positively affect your one-to-one relationships, both personal and professional. You have tended to overlay parental issues on partners.

Jupiter and Saturn activate contradictory areas this year. Saturn in Pisces indicates a serious and hardworking time, when your vitality is lowered and your sphere of influence diminished. Jupiter offers public recognition and sudden opportunities through your work, as you are drawn to involvement in some progressive organization. The challenge: to make sure you give yourself whatever you need to nourish yourself, while you take on just enough power and position to be effective out in the world. Total self-absorption and isolation will leave you anxious and melancholy; too much public involvement will leave you drained and overwhelmed. Narrow the focus of your efforts; simplify your everyday life.

Uranus influences your 12th house during 1995. Healing of old emotional traumas occurs suddenly through an unusual spiritual discipline. People from your past (even other lives) show up in your life or in your dreams. Opportunities appear to resolve unfinished issues with them.   © *Gretchen Lawlor 1994*

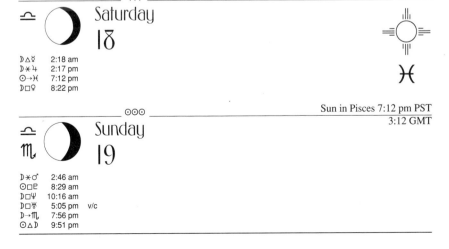

♎ **Saturday 18**

☽△♅	2:18 am
☽✶♃	2:17 pm
☉→♓	7:12 pm
☽□♀	8:22 pm

♓

Sun in Pisces 7:12 pm PST
3:12 GMT

♎ ♏ **Sunday 19**

☽✶♂	2:46 am	
☉□♇	8:29 am	
☽□♆	10:16 am	
☽□♅	5:05 pm	v/c
☽→♏	7:56 pm	
☉△☽	9:51 pm	

Februar

  Montag
20

D□☿   7:23 am
D△♄   6:57 pm

"Inside This Shell of Mine"
© *Nancy Bright 1990*

----------- ♂♂♂ -----------

 Dienstag
21

D⚹♀   4:31 am
D□♂   4:54 am
D⚹♇   1:46 am
D⚹♅   8:35 pm   v/c
D→♐ 11:14 pm

----------- ☿☿☿ -----------

 Mittwoch
22

D♂♇ 12:12 am
☉□D   5:05 am
D⚹♅ 12:38 pm
DPrG   6:18 pm
D♂♃   9:50 pm
D□♄ 10:30 pm

----------- ♄♄♄ -----------   Waning Half Moon in ♐ Sagittarius 5:05 am PST, 13:05 GMT

 Donnerstag
23

D△♂   6:41 am   v/c

----------- ♀♀♀ -----------

 Freitag
24

D→♑   2:12 am
☉⚹D 11:56 am

All aspects in Pacific Standard Time; add 3 hours for EST; add 8 hours for GMT

Solitude endures longer than leaves.
Not as long as trees.

© *Sudie Rakusin 1984*

California Poppy   *Eschscholtzia californica*

In the depths of the year, the brilliant orange California poppy brings us the expansive sunfire of new visions in a framework of centered tranquillity. When prepared and used as tea or tincture, she calms safely, and encourages imaginative introspection and visualization. Not as strong a sedative as her poppy cousins, but very effective for relief of worry and sleeplessness. An inspiring presence in the garden as a meditation companion, or when used internally. Seeds are now increasingly available. Don't gather in the wild. Replenish the earth with this special plant which can grow as an annual anywhere and as a perennial in mild climates.

© *Billie Potts 1994*

♑ ☾ ♄♄♄ **Samstag**
25

♇△⚷	1:32 am
☾✶♄	1:53 am
☾☌♀	7:42 pm
☾☌♇	7:59 pm
♀△⚷	9:20 pm
♀☌♇	11:07 pm

⊙⊙⊙

♑ ☾ **Sonntag**
♒
26

☾☌♅	2:58 am	v/c
☾→♒	5:15 am	
☾✶♇	6:16 am	

Beyond Resistance: Surviving Incest Into Action

(As I remember something happened to me, pieces fall into place: I used to freeze when adults were invasive to the children in my care. I couldn't find words. Why didn't I protect them?)

1
Resist: I eat.
I resist my legs parting wide
turn of foot leading thigh
open.
Close my mouth around another bite.

2
The city blares.
Metal waterfall
of scrap dealer next door.
My world is cement and rules.
I resist returning calls
from caring friends. Diversions
of my attention
from the tightness in my belly
from the pressure on my chest
raw choking back of throat
burning in vagina, like semen.

© *Sudie Rakusin 1987*

    (Why did I say that?
    How do I know about semen?)

3
Find the grace for a move
   to the country.
Study:
Body truths, frozen trapped
ready cautious thawing wary.
Memory comes in trusting self:
    eat when hungry.
    sleep when tired.
    listen when scared.
    cry.
Memory comes;
my vision
and my voice
clear.

4
She is two and turns her back
as you pat her on the head.
"NO" escapes my be-polite muddle,
explodes don't – offend fear.
It is for us both.

5
If survival is an act of resistance,*
then by my memory
I have already changed the world.

         ¤ *Grace Silvia 1992*

*"Survival is an Act of Resistance" <u>*We Speak in Code*</u>
Melanie Kaye Kantrowitz, credited Meridel LeSueur,
<u>*Motheroot*</u>, 1980.

III. REMEMBERING / GRIEF MOON

© *Vicki Moser & Marianna L. Crawford 1993*
Ceramic sculpture and poetry

somedays i resist
  opening into you
    allowing you to nourish me
      with your potent arms
       but when i let go
        you cradle me and gently caress my head.
       my heart sobs in grief
        for the lost days
         of innocence and harmony
         that i knew like a lover
          long long ago
           when this chalice was whole
            and swelling with creative dreams.

fevrier

"tatterdemalion"

≈ **lundi**

27

☽ ☌ ☿   12:48 am
☽ ⚹ ♃   4:53 am
☽ ☍ ♂   10:45 am   v/c

♂♂♂

≈
♓ **mardi**

28

☽ → ♓   9:17 am
☽ ◻ ♇   10:20 am

☿☿☿

♓ **mercredi**

1

mars

☉ ☌ ☽   3:49 am
☽ ◻ ♃   10:08 am
☽ ☌ ♄   11:07 am
♀ ☌ ♅   2:19 pm
☿ ⚹ ♃   4:58 pm

♃♃♃

New Moon in ♓ Pisces 3:49 am PST, 11:49 GMT

♓
♈ **jeudi**

2

☽ ⚹ ♆   5:44 am
☽ ⚹ ♅   1:26 pm   v/c
♀ → ≈   2:12 pm
☽ → ♈   3:31 pm
☽ ⚹ ♀   3:39 pm
☽ △ ♇   4:38 pm

♀♀♀

♈ **vendredi**

3

♀ ⚹ ♇   2:33 am
☿ ☍ ♂   1:11 pm
♇ sR   2:19 pm
☽ △ ♃   6:09 pm
☽ △ ♂   9:24 pm
☽ ⚹ ☿   10:23 pm

All aspects in Pacific Standard Time; add 3 hours for EST; add 8 hours for GMT

tatterdemalion*

© *Red Raven 1993*

*Tatterdemalion means tattered in shreds, being in a decayed state or condition – the state of my spirit before women's spirituality.

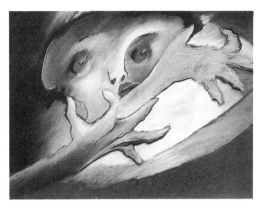

Accepting the Truth I Forgot
© *Ann Hemdahl-Owen 1992*

buried stone child
brave in that dense darkness
dreaming safe stories
wrapped in illusions
illusions of mother love
illusions of father's wisdom
carefully dreamed
in fitful night sleeps
in migraine daymares.
yellow dotted swiss
rickrack and lace
steaming cookies
and the purple pedal car
...a "loved child" illusion.
everyday
they tore up your dreams
they tied you
with them
arms wound round
bound
with their pain
secured
in cross stitched hates.
digging charred shards
in your cold bed
i find
your rusty bedspring halo
...unearthing your light

ħħħ

 ♈ samedi
4

☽□♆   2:38 pm
☽□♅ 10:52 pm   v/c
☉□♃ 11:20 pm

☉☉☉

 ♈ dimanche
♉ 5

☽→♉ 12:51 am
☽□♀   7:07 am
ħApG   2:40 pm
☉♂ħ   5:33 pm

marzo

〇 lunes
6

》》》

D ✶ ♄   6:48 am
D □ ♂   7:09 am
☉ ✶ D   7:52 am
D □ ☿   3:46 pm

♂♂♂

〇
Ⅱ

martes
7

D △ ♆   2:29 am
D △ ♅   11:07 am   v/c
D → Ⅱ   12:56 pm
D ☍ ♇   2:09 pm

"Healing After Abortion"

☿☿☿

Ⅱ

miercoles
8

D △ ♀   2:04 am
D ApG   7:02 am
D ☍ ♃   6:28 pm
D ✶ ♂   6:49 pm
D □ ♄   8:12 pm

♃♃♃

Ⅱ

jueves
9

☉ □ D   2:15 am
♂ △ ♃   10:25 am
D △ ♅   11:47 am   v/c

♀♀♀

Waxing Half Moon in Ⅱ Gemini 2:15 am PST, 10:15 GMT

Ⅱ
♋

viernes
10

D → ♋   1:41 am

All aspects in Pacific Standard Time; add 3 hours for EST; add 8 hours for GMT

□ Denise A. Fortier 1992

After a Miscarriage My Prayer is a Stone's Lonely Hum

In this small room in the City of Angels there are no candles
wrapped in cobras of clay, no Goddess
to prescribe a cure, to tell me: <u>Walk in circles</u>.

It is winter. Where could I find a river
that would accept me like a Goddess? People say
there are no seasons

in these suburbs, but I imagine seasons do exist, subtle chords
rippling like the leaves of summer corn, following light.

I ache for zucchini or tomato to spill fruit over dirt
but in January the time is more right for cutting back.
How can I desire

anything to bloom when even the feet of angels are bound
like roots and cracked with cold.

Of course seasons exist here. We'll pay our small debts
of attention or miss the changes, the verbena blossoming in sand.

¤ *Suzanne Ghiglia 1990*

_____ ᚻᚻᚻ _____

♋ sabado
II

☽△♄   8:50 am
☉△☽   7:20 pm

_____ ☉☉☉ _____

♋
♌ domingo
12

☽☌♆   2:50 am
☽☌♅   11:11 am   v/c
☽→♌   12:29 pm
☽△♇   1:36 pm

*"Lament for the Unborn Dead,
Safe In the Arms of the Dark Mother"*
¤ *Nicola Beechsquirrel 1991*

March

The earth cracks:
The women walk in and out:
Underneath is grief.

□ *Zetta Bear 1992*

 DDD

♌ ☽ Monday
13

☽☍♀	12:45 pm
☽♂♂	2:36 pm
☽△♃	4:22 pm v/c
☉☍♅	11:31 pm

♂♂♂

♌
♍ ☽ Tuesday
14

♀☍♂	7:01 am
☿→♓	1:36 pm
☽→♍	7:55 pm
☽☍♅	8:41 pm
☽☐♇	8:56 pm
☿☐♇	11:09 pm

☿☿☿

♍ ☽ Wednesday
15

♀⚹♃	5:55 am
☉⚹♆	6:53 am
☽☐♃	10:23 pm

♃♃♃

♍ ◯ Thursday
16

☽☍♄	12:39 am
♄PrG	1:37 pm
☽△♆	3:52 pm
☉☍☽	5:27 pm
☽△♅	11:27 pm v/c

Full Moon in ♍ Virgo 5:27 pm PST
1:27 GMT

♀♀♀

♍
♎ ◯ Friday
17

☽→♎	12:19 am
☽⚹♇	1:15 am
☽⚹♂	11:05 pm

All aspects in Pacific Standard Time; add 3 hours for EST; add 8 hours for GMT

Remember Everything: the Beauteous, the Sorrowful

Passionflower   *Passiflora incarnata*

Enjoy the splendid passionflower which tranquilizes without depressing the spirit and promotes soul retrieval. Passionflower helps us recall memories and dreams, even difficult ones, and aids us in surviving losses, hard remembrances, and the deepest grief. Teas and tinctures of passionflowers and top leaves are mildly sedating, but do not down out the central nervous system. They bring quietude and inspirit feelings of hope. Passionflower gives long-term, non-addicting support to wimmin withdrawing from caffeine, nicotine, alcohol, and other disruptive drugs. Bless the homespace with an outdoor trellis of vining passionflower or a large indoor container where winters are cold.

© *Billie Potts 1994*

ħħħ

♎ 🌙 Saturday
18

☽✶♃	1:52 am
☽△♀	7:47 am
☽□♆	6:43 pm

☉☉☉

♎ 🌙 Sunday
♏ 19

☽□♅	2:11 am	v/c
☽→♏	2:53 am	
☽△♅	3:27 pm	

Spring

The sudden flower
Stands ice-encrusted,
Rooted in snow,
And laughs in the teeth of the wind.
"I am Spring!" she says.

"I will kill you," the storm replies.
"I will shatter your frozen petals and
Scatter them on the glee of my destroying."

"Not so," she counters.
"Your very ice which holds me
Holds me pure, holds me strong.
Because I stand, I remain before your face,
And I am the gateway
Beyond the barriers of Chaos."

The wind howls again,
But with the sound of mourning.
The flower clings still to the snow.   *© Francesca Thoman 1992*

© Red Raven 1993

Spring Equinox

Spring Equinox is a time when the day and night force are equal, when plants begin to burst forth from the earth, when leaves appear on the trees, and the movement of insects is felt again. Spring is the time when Persephone returns from the underworld as a young girl, and mother and daughter play together out in the fields and usher in the new growth. It is a time for each of us to honor the child within and give voice to that child. It is also a time for each of us to cleanse our bodies and spirits in preparation for the rebirth.

The celebration of Easter occurs close to the time of this equinox. *Oestre* or *Eostar* was a feast of the goddess Ishtar/Astarte/Esther and celebrated her rebirth. The egg was used as a symbol for Eostar as it represented the birth of the Goddess and of all nature.

Prior to the equinox it is important that each woman do some individual cleansing, including a spring fast, and colonic or herbal enemas. Letting go of old material in the body precipitates the letting go of old emotions stored up in the dark of winter. The night before the equinox, or that day, it is good to do a special sweat.   *© Marcia Starck 1993, printed and excerpted from*
Women's Medicine Ways: Cross-Cultural Rites of Passage
with permission from The Crossing Press.

◻ *Rachel Bachman 1993*

Fierce Mary

you chopped down my tree house
but i am rebuilding.
you told me to wear a shirt and talk softly.
but i am naked and i shout.
i have a voice and ideas to birth
i have a life and no one will take it from me again.
i am your worst nightmare because i refuse to be silent any longer.
i will spread out my wings, my body. i will give voice to what i see
i will fight but not with strength.
i will haunt you because you do not want
to see me.

März

♏   **Montag**
     20

☽□♂	1:03 am
☽PrG	5:14 am
☽△♄	6:54 am
☉⚹♅	9:09 am
☽□♀	2:26 pm
☉→♈	6:15 pm
☽⚹♆	8:53 pm

Equinox

Sun in Aries 6:15 pm PST
2:15 GMT

♏ ♐   **Dienstag**
     21

☽⚹♅	4:23 am	v/c
☽→♐	4:58 am	
☉△☽	5:46 am	
☽☌♇	5:50 am	
☉△♇	6:45 am	
☽□♅	11:45 pm	

♐   **Mittwoch**
     22

☽△♂	3:07 am	
☽☌♃	6:32 am	
☽□♄	9:36 am	
☽⚹♀	9:25 pm	v/c

♐ ♑   **Donnerstag**
     23

| ☽→♑ | 7:32 am |
| ☉□☽ | 12:11 pm |

Waning Half Moon in ♑ Capricorn 12:11 pm PST, 20:11 GMT

♑   **Freitag**
     24

♂sD	9:18 am
☽⚹♅	9:19 am
♅□♃	12:35 pm
☽⚹♄	1:10 pm

All aspects in Pacific Standard Time; add 3 hours for EST; add 8 hours for GMT

Year at a glance for ARIES ♈ (Mar. 20–Apr. 19)

In 1995 the theme for Aries is completion. A major phase in your life ends as Saturn journeys through your 12th house (early 1994 through early 1996). The challenge is to celebrate your successes, face your failures, and free yourself of the encumbrances of your old life. If you cannot do this, you will find yourself awash in the accumulated results of past failures. It is not a time to start anything of major significance. Activities that used to work for you no longer do; old ways of handling people no longer work. An old skin must be shed; this is less painful to do now than it was last year.

To succeed at this closure you need a source of spiritual strength, though Aries doesn't easily sit still in meditation. Walking, dancing, hiking – these moving meditations help you shift from fear to power. Another way to contact your strength is through volunteering your skills to social causes or working with service institutions. Your energy will fluctuate. It is a time of waiting, of dreaming and inner exploration.

With Jupiter and Pluto both in Sagittarius during 1995 your perspective on life opens up. Jupiter brings a burst of optimism and an ability to look at your life from a more detached philosophical viewpoint. Pluto manifests through crises, transforming and deepening your attitudes through contact with faith, philosophy, or politics. A foreigner or someone contacted during a journey is an important teacher for you this year. From this experience you may decide to take on advanced studies in some philosophical or political field.

Unusual friendships appear which bring out your eccentric, unconventional self. It's a good time for you to explore group activities where you will be introduced to ideas or insights which will set your life moving in exciting new directions. © *Gretchen Lawlor 1994*

♑
♒

ℏℏℏ

Samstag
25

☽♂♆   2:54 am
☽♂♅   10:49 am   v/c
☽→♒   11:11 am
☽⚹♇   11:60 am
♀♂♄   7:52 pm
☉⚹☽   7:58 pm

○○○

♒

Sonntag
26

☽☍♂   10:20 am
☽⚹♃   2:07 pm

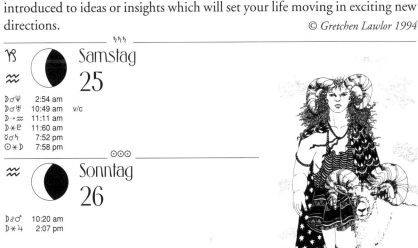

© *Sudie Rakusin 1989*

One night
It came back
My memory
Tall and erect
In the form of The Pedophile
Walking through my dream door
The spark of recognition in both our eyes

How dare you return at night
When I am alone, dormant
Half-dressed
You pick your hour by the light of my insecurities
Don't you?
Just as you pluck your small, powerless victims
From the cocoon of innocent trust
How dare you return
Uninvited
I will not give you the power to hurt me again
I am in this adult body
able and alert
My child has given way
dormant
inside of me
But it is the adult-I that you must reckon with

Time turns your child victims into
Angry
Adult
Survivors
Recognize me?

Medusa Unwound   © *Judith Anderson 1993*
photo by J. Colando

The Power Of Common Words

I am called lady, smile sweetly, be nice, cross legs, tighten ass.
I am called hag, smell of cunty sweat, spot clothes, persist hairy.
I am called woman, prattle softly, marry a man, do the expected.
I am called silly, giggle, cry easily, listen well, act vulnerable.
I am called bitch, know what's right, speak directly, stay specific.
I am called penis envy, assume a businesslike attitude, be assertive.
I am called invitation, eat a solo dinner, walk alone in a park.
I am called victim, encounter difficulties, live hurt, wish for mercy.
I am called mother, offer nurturance, give acceptance, remain loving.
I am called whore, howl in orgasm, fierce in heat, appear sexy.
I am called witch, delight in thunderstorms, exist as a catalyst.
I am called stupid, give birth to sons, daughters, kiss tiny fingers.
I am called old lady, hold wisdom of years, bear gifts for generations.

Part 1 of 2 © Mari Susan Selby 1993

mars

_____ ☽☽☽ _____

How many creative geniuses are locked up in mental hospitals? Where do the homeless people come from? They come from the raw end of the mental health system which is corrupt, totally corrupt and rotten to the core.
© Roxanne Firewind 1989

♒
♓
lundi
27

☽♂♀	3:50 pm	v/c
☽→♓	4:19 pm	
☽□♇	5:07 pm	
♀→♓	9:11 pm	

_____ ♂♂♂ _____

♓
mardi
28

♀□♇	5:56 am	
☿⚸♇	1:32 pm	
☽□♃	8:16 pm	

_____ ☿☿☿ _____

♓
♈
mercredi
29

☽♂♄	12:49 am	
☽♂☿	11:44 am	
☽✶♆	2:41 pm	
☽✶♅	11:20 pm	v/c
☽→♈	11:27 pm	

_____ ♃♃♃ _____

♈
jeudi
30

☽△♇	12:13 am	
☿✶♆	9:28 am	
☉♂☽	6:10 pm	

_____ ♀♀♀ _____

New Moon in ♈ Aries 6:10 pm PST
2:10 GMT

♈
vendredi
31

☽△♂	12:53 am	
☽△♃	4:38 am	
☽□♆	11:55 pm	v/c

All aspects, except April 2, in Pacific Standard Time; add 3 hours for EST; add 8 hours for GMT

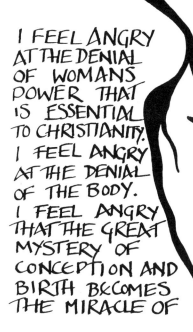

I FEEL ANGRY AT THE DENIAL OF WOMANS POWER THAT IS ESSENTIAL TO CHRISTIANITY. I FEEL ANGRY AT THE DENIAL OF THE BODY. I FEEL ANGRY THAT THE GREAT MYSTERY OF CONCEPTION AND BIRTH BECOMES THE MIRACLE OF THE FATHER(S) IN THE IMMACULATE CONCEPTION. I AM ANGRY THAT SEX DIDN'T GET A LOOKIN. I AM ANGRY THAT YOU STOLE MY MYTHS AND MYSTERYS AND TURNED THEM UPSIDE DOWN. I AM ANGRY THAT YOU SHUN (YET LONG FOR) MY BELLY AND BREAST

© Kirsty O'Connor 1992

♈ ☿	🌑	**samedi** 1		**avril**

♃sR 3:19 am
♅→♒ 4:07 am
☽→♉ 9:00 am
☽□♅ 9:00 am
☽⚹♀ 8:44 pm
☿→♈ 11:30 pm
☿⚹♅ 11:48 pm

♉	🌑	**dimanche** 2

☿△♇ 5:15 am
☽□♂ 12:60 pm
☽⚹♄ 10:29 pm

Daylight Savings Time Begins 2:00 am PST

abril

☽☽☽

♉
♊

lunes
3

☽△♆	12:32 pm	v/c
☉△♂	5:37 pm	
☽→♊	9:50 pm	
☽△♅	9:59 pm	
☽☍♇	10:31 pm	

♂♂♂

♊

martes
4

☽⚹♉	6:17 am
☽□♀	4:43 pm

☿☿☿

♊

miercoles
5

☽⚹♂	2:08 am	
☽ApG	3:08 am	
☉⚹☽	4:44 am	
☽☍♃	4:59 am	
☉△♃	7:51 am	
☽□♄	11:46 am	v/c

♃♃♃

♊
♋

jueves
6

☽→♋	10:41 am

♀♀♀

♋

viernes
7

☽□♉	6:46 am
☽△♀	12:11 pm
☉□☽	10:36 pm

Waxing Half Moon in ♋ Cancer 10:36 pm PDT
5:36 GMT (April 8)

All aspects in Pacific Daylight Time; add 3 hours for EDT; add 7 hours for GMT

At the moment my anger against
my inner child vanished, the child
herself could finally express her anger.

© *Marja de Vries 1992*

ᚼᚼᚼ

♋
♌

sabado
8

☽△♄	12:41 am	
☽☌♆	1:25 pm	v/c
☽→♌	10:16 pm	
☽☌♅	10:39 pm	
☽△♇	10:45 pm	

☉☉☉

♌

domingo
9

☿△♂	3:24 pm
♀□♃	3:42 pm
☿△♃	10:35 pm

April

♌ _DDD_

Monday
10

☽☌♂	2:27 am
☽△♃	3:26 am
☽△♅	4:21 am
☿ApG	8:15 am
♅⚹♇	9:09 am
☉△☽	1:12 pm v/c

♌
♍ _♂♂♂_

Tuesday
11

☽→♍	6:40 am
☽□♇	7:02 am

♍ _☿☿☿_

Wednesday
12

☽□♃	9:46 am
♂△♃	10:06 am
☽☍♀	4:16 pm
☽☍♄	5:18 pm

♍
♎ _♃♃♃_

Thursday
13

☽△♆	3:39 am v/c
♀☌♄	5:15 am
☽→♎	11:21 am
☽⚹♇	11:37 am
☽△♅	11:50 am

♎ _♀♀♀_

Friday
14

☉☌♅	5:50 am
♀☍♇	9:51 am
☽⚹♃	12:44 pm
☽⚹♂	1:37 pm
☿□♆	9:47 pm

All aspects in Pacific Daylight Time; add 3 hours for EDT; add 7 hours for GMT

Telling

your throat
in childhood
sealed off in the
shame you knew
and imagined

imagine being

the tight wrap
of the past
comes undone

you take a truthful pen
and feed the hunger

you have moved
from the stone house

playing with the hidden
you in fact
have a knack
for lifting the ban
on sealed secrets

◻ *Julia Doughty 1993*

◻ *Carole Shaw 1993*

Do You Hear Me Now?

♎︎ ◯ **Saturday**
♏︎ **15**

☉☍☽	5:09 am	
☽□♆	5:53 am	
☽☍♅	7:14 am	v/c
☽→♏︎	1:14 pm	
☽□♅	1:45 pm	
☉□♆	4:08 pm	

Full Moon in ♎︎ Libra 5:09 am PDT, 12:09 GMT
Partial Lunar Eclipse (.111 magn.) 5:18 PDT

♏︎ ◯ **Sunday**
16

| ☽□♂ | 3:24 pm |
| ☽△♄ | 9:37 pm |

April

_ DDD _

♏
♐

Montag
17

♉→♈	12:55 am	
☽PrG	1:15 am	
☽△♀	4:44 am	
♉□♅	4:47 am	
☽✶♆	6:37 am	v/c
☽→♐	1:52 pm	
☽☌♇	1:59 pm	
☽✶♅	2:26 pm	

AIDS eradicates
a culture
a thought
a possibility
most don't want to conceive
STOP AIDS
excerpt ▭ Laura Irene Wayne 1991

_ ♂♂♂ _

♐

Dienstag
18

♀✶♆	4:06 am
☽☌♃	2:07 pm
☽△♂	4:54 pm
☽□♄	10:43 pm

_ ☿☿☿ _

♐
♑

Mittwoch
19

☽□♀	10:00 am	
☉△☽	1:47 pm	v/c
☽→♑	2:55 pm	

_ ♃♃♃ _

♑

Donnerstag
20

☽△♉	1:34 am
☉→♉	6:22 am
☉□♅	3:55 pm
♇R→♏	7:52 pm

Sun in Taurus 6:22 am PDT, 13:22 GMT

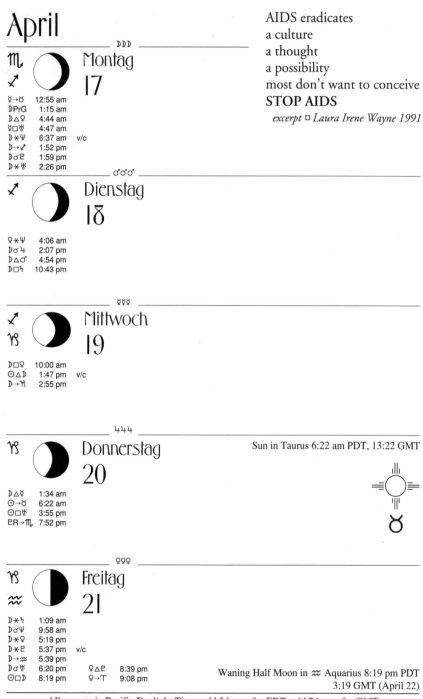

♉

_ ♀♀♀ _

♑
♒

Freitag
21

☽✶♄	1:09 am			
☽☌♆	9:58 am			
☽✶♀	5:19 pm			
☽✶♇	5:37 pm	v/c		
☽→♒	5:39 pm			
☽☌♅	6:20 pm	♀△♇	8:39 pm
☉□☽	8:19 pm	♀→♈	9:08 pm

Waning Half Moon in ♒ Aquarius 8:19 pm PDT
3:19 GMT (April 22)

All aspects in Pacific Daylight Time; add 3 hours for EDT; add 7 hours for GMT

Year at a glance for TAURUS ♉ (Apr. 20–May 20)

For several years you have felt restless and unsettled, as you've looked for ways to free yourself from professional responsibilities. You have recently done, or will soon do, something to radically alter your vocation or public self. Idealism or friendships influence your decision. If you wish to stay in your present field, channel itchy rebelliousness into experimentation, innovation, or collaboration.

Saturn brings into focus ambitions you have been trying to realize for years. Everything could fall into place quite suddenly, by working collectively with peers and without bosses. Frustration with limitations or demands of associates should be dealt with rather than avoided; your rewards come from teamwork this year.

For years, partnerships have been the setting for your significant personal transformations. By making changes in yourself, you have recently reached a deeper level of commitment in a significant one-to-one relationship. For some Taureans an intense relationship will finally be over.

In 1995 Pluto begins a twelve-year transit of your 8th house, setting off crises related to shared resources. Changes in the values and/or financial situation of someone close affects you profoundly. You could receive an unexpected windfall, perhaps an inheritance. With Jupiter's contact in 1995, insights into your own psychological makeup help you to wield your power better. You are less controlling or manipulative of others. You are becoming more sensitive to the undercurrents around you, and to the hidden or unexpressed feelings of others. You are fascinated with mysteries, metaphysics, or psychology – anything that helps you to understand the deep impressions you are picking up.

Chiron's emphasis is upon healing old traumas to your self-esteem incurred during childhood. Play therapy (maybe just more time to play) brings out a sunnier, more lighthearted self.

© Gretchen Lawlor 1994

♒ Samstag
22

♀✶♅	5:12 am
☽□♅	2:02 pm
♄♂♄	5:33 pm
☽✶♃	7:20 pm

☉☉☉

♒
♓ Sonntag
23

☽♂♂	12:53 am	
☽□♇	10:43 pm	v/c
☽→♓	10:51 pm	

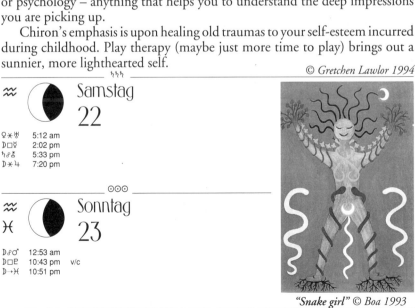

"Snake girl" © Boa 1993

avril

OUT OF SILENCE

♓ ☽☽☽ **lundi**
24

☉⚹☽　5:57 am

♓ ♂♂♂ **mardi**
25

☽□♃　1:33 am
☽⚹♅　6:25 am
☽♂♄　1:24 pm
☽⚹♆　10:15 pm

♓ ♈ ☿☿☿ **mercredi**
26

☿□♂　1:27 am
☽△♇　6:27 am　v/c
☽→♈　6:42 am
☽⚹♅　7:33 am
☽♂♀　5:56 pm
☿△♌　10:35 pm

♈ ♃♃♃ **jeudi**
27

☿⚹♄　6:31 am
☽△♃　10:15 am
♆sR　10:36 am
☽△♂　7:46 pm

♈ ♉ ♀♀♀ **vendredi**
28

☽□♆　8:08 am　v/c
☽→♉　4:54 pm
☽□♅　5:48 pm

All aspects in Pacific Daylight Time; add 3 hours for EDT; add 7 hours for GMT

Healing from Incest

Emerging from a ball of clay –
from under my fingers,
her face takes form.
stares at me
and I understand
and embrace
the enormous power of my rage
¤ *Christine Pierce 1993*

Rosemary *Rosmarinus officinalis*

Shining blue rosemary flowers stimulate energy, awakenings of conscious-ness, and our ability to remember clearly. Weak tea of flowering rosemary improves liver health. The liver is often the storehouse of unresolved hurt and anger. Hand and foot baths of flowering sprigs provide channels of release and emotional expression. Baths or vapor steams with rosemary flowers are so clearing that body and soul often reconnect after the discovery of old trauma through the use of rosemary flowers. All centers of our being feel toned and eager to initiate new undertakings.

Infuse rosemary flowers into vinegar for salad dressings, or for a tonic splash. The flowering tops, infused into olive oil, can provide skin and scalp healing benefits year-round. Rosemary is sacred to the great earth and sea goddesses of Mediterranean cultures. Dry the flowering tops on screens and store for cleansing ritual and protection.   © *Billie Potts 1994*

ħħħ

♉   ● samedi
29

⊙☌☽   10:37 am
☿△♆   5:33 pm

New Moon in ♉ Taurus 10:37 am PDT, 17:37 GMT
Annular Solar Eclipse (6 min. 37 sec.) 10:32 am PDT

⊙⊙⊙

♉   ◑ dimanche
30

☽□♂   8:52 am
☽⚹ħ   11:25 am
☽△♆   7:55 pm

My thighs are thick and thunderous!
My waist is wide and wonderous!

My belly's rounded room
Holds the full and glowing moon,

The mountains of my breasts
Are a living treasure chest,

My hips so soft and wide
Hold the universe inside,

My legs are mighty stumps
To support my mountainous rump.

Oh what a lucky chance
To be blessed with such expanse!

To take my womanly stance
In this universal dance.

Now some would try to strip and starve me
Some would try to mold and carve me

But nothing is more belittling
Than that narrow-minded whittling!

It is not my bound duty
To befit the little beauty

My thighs are thick and thunderous!
My waist is wide and wonderous!

This body that was sent to me
Is the form that it is meant to be!

Aho!   *Joules 1992*

V. RECLAIMING THE BODY MOON

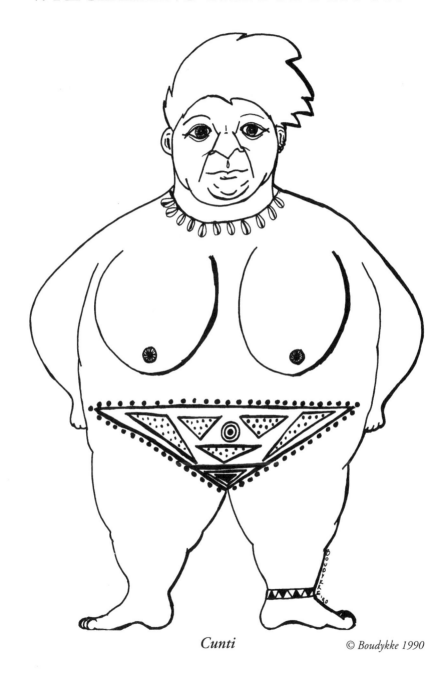

Cunti

mayo

© *Marja de Vries 1985*

 DDD

♉
♊   lunes

1

D♂♉ 12:26 am
D☍♇ 4:23 am v/c
D→♊ 4:54 am
D△♅ 5:51 am

Beltane

♂♂♂

♊ martes

2

☿☍♇ 4:12 am
D✶♀ 6:19 am
☿→♊ 8:19 am
D☍♃ 9:07 am
☿△♅ 3:20 pm
DApG 5:45 pm
D✶♂ 11:24 pm

☿☿☿

♊
♋   miercoles

3

D□♄ 12:39 am v/c
♀△♃ 7:57 am
D→♋ 5:46 pm

♃♃♃

♋   jueves

4

♅sR 8:45 pm
☉✶D 10:36 pm

♀♀♀

♋   viernes

5

D□♀ 1:58 am
D△♄ 1:39 pm
D☍♆ 9:05 pm

All aspects in Pacific Daylight Time; add 3 hours for EDT; add 7 hours for GMT

© Sudie Rakusin 1984

Beltane or May Day

Beltane was another of the ancient fire festivals in Europe. The Beltane fires and the Maypole celebrate fertility and the earth's ripe abundance. Persephone comes of age and is ready to experience her sexuality. Lovers sleep outdoors and make love in the fields to insure the fertility of the crops. Dances are done around the Maypole during the day, and at night lovers jump over the Beltane fires.

All these rites were to insure the fertility of nature, just as the fires were purificatory and were believed to protect against pestilence, plague, and epidemics.

Om

In a world
Where women
Do not kiss
On TV, billboards or
In moving pictures
Where there are
People unaware that
We exist
As possibility or fact
Your lips are
Sucking me
Out of my
Hiding places
You are
Loving me
Wide open
We are
Uncoiled
Energy
Kinetic
Flowing
Power
We are
Endless time
Möbius strip
We are never
An idea
Already formed
We are only
This right now
Your deep eyes
Passion glassy
Looking into mine
My forehead pressed
To yours as you
Nurse my breast
An urgent bliss
A shifting holy
Celebration

Creation

© Margaret De Maria 1993

In a world
Where some in weakness
Wish to kill us
For our strength
Your hands are
Reaching way inside me
Midwife
Sacred water bearer
Always giving birth
We are singing
The one verse
The universe.

© Diana Cohen 1990

Tattoos I Want To Get, And Why:

A red Chinese-style dragon, preferably on my ass, because a dragon is life and a dragon is fire and it seems only fair to warn people,

Celtic knotwork at the base of my spine, because it is gorgeous and would hurt enough to make me remember it,

A small sign reading "Burn This," haven't decided where to put that one, just in case the new witchfinders are more inept than the old ones,

A snake twisting around my ankle, to remind me that knowledge isn't evil no matter who tells me different,

Two cobalt wings on my shoulder blades, for those times when sheer anger isn't enough, and fury is necessary.

© *Erica Owens 1993*

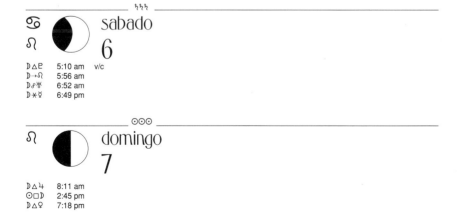

♋
♌   ● sabado
6

♈♈♈

☽△♇   5:10 am   v/c
☽→♌   5:56 am
☽☍♅   6:52 am
☽⚹☿   6:49 pm

♌   ◑ domingo
7

☉☉☉

☽△♃   8:11 am
☉□☽   2:45 pm
☽△♀   7:18 pm

Waxing Half Moon in ♌ Leo 2:45 pm PDT, 21:45 GMT

May

♌ ♍ | Monday 8
ⅅⅅⅅ

☽☌♂	2:04 am
♀⊼⅋	11:23 am
☽□♇	2:44 pm v/c
☽→♍	3:34 pm

"Full/ness Moon"
¤ *Debby Earthdaughter 1993*

♍ | Tuesday 9
♂♂♂

☽□♅	9:38 am
☽□♃	3:49 pm

♍ ♎ | Wednesday 10
☿☿☿

☉△☽	2:41 am
☽☍♄	7:53 am
☽△♆	1:41 pm
☽✳♇	8:38 pm v/c
☉△⅋	9:06 pm
☽→♎	9:31 pm
☽△♅	10:19 pm

♎ | Thursday 11
♃♃♃

☽△♅	6:36 pm
☽✳♃	7:42 pm
♀△♂	11:46 pm

♎ ♏ | Friday 12
♀♀♀

♅☍♃	9:38 am
☽✳♂	3:00 pm
☽☍♀	3:56 pm
☽□♆	4:31 pm v/c
♀□♆	10:59 pm
☽→♏	11:54 pm

All aspects in Pacific Daylight Time; add 3 hours for EDT; add 7 hours for GMT

□ Jennifer Lynn Shafer 1993

ħħħ

♏  ☽ Saturday
13

☽□♅ 12:38 am
☉⚹♄ 9:52 am

☉☉☉

♏
♐

Sunday
14

☽△♄ 12:10 pm
☉☍☽ 1:49 pm
☽□♂ 4:42 pm
☽⚹♆ 4:49 pm
☽☌♇ 11:00 pm   v/c
☽→♐ 11:59 pm

Lunar Beltane
Full Moon in ♏ Scorpio 1:49 pm PDT, 20:49 GMT

Mai

♐ ## Montag
15

☽⚹♅ 12:41 am
☽PrG 8:23 am
☽♂♃ 7:50 pm

♐
♑ ## Dienstag
16

☽☍♅ 12:58 am
☽□♄ 11:58 am
☉△♆ 12:18 pm
♀→♉ 4:23 pm
☽△♂ 5:36 pm v/c
☽→♑ 11:37 pm

♑ ## Mittwoch
17

☽△♀ 12:15 am
♀□♅ 12:36 am
☉□♂ 6:58 pm
♇sD 7:57 pm

♑ ## Donnerstag
18

☽⚹♄ 12:47 pm
☽♂♆ 5:02 pm
☉△☽ 8:52 pm
☽⚹♇ 11:27 pm v/c

♑
♒ ## Freitag
19

☽→♒ 12:40 am
☽♂♅ 1:20 am
☽□♀ 5:54 am
☽⚹♃ 9:09 pm

All aspects in Pacific Daylight Time; add 3 hours for EDT; add 7 hours for GMT

Year at a glance for GEMINI ♊ (May 21–June 20)

Pluto begins a twelve-year transit of your house of relationships in 1995. This first year, particularly with Jupiter's influence, brings surprising developments. If you aren't already involved, someone significant will enter your life. If you are in a relationship, it needs to deepen, or it will blow apart in the next few years. All your one-to-one interactions are intense, not only with mates, but with business partners and those with whom you consult. Whether they stay in your life depends on whether you thrive on intensity and are willing to change.

Saturn in Pisces continues to influence your vocation. Until early 1996 you will be working very hard, dedicated to manifesting professional ambitions you have had for years. This is a time of culmination, when you are given public respect and plenty of responsibility. It is always difficult for Gemini to focus exclusively on one thing. You need the freedom to bring a variety of talents to your work arena, and to create your own schedule. Work with institutions, work involving spiritual values, or work for social causes will be most satisfying.

Uranus leaves Capricorn and moves on to Aquarius, where it sets off a seven-year wave of independence and originality. For Gemini this need for experimentation is acted out through politics, religion, or advanced education. Your thoughts are progressive, you have profound insights – even genius – to share with the world. You have the ability to be a catalyst in education, politics, or religion but will need discipline, or the energy could be wasted in unreasonable stubbornness and impractical eccentricity. Your thoughts are ahead of their time; you will need to be diplomatic or tactful in how you present them. There will be unexpected opportunities to teach or publish.

© *Gretchen Lawlor 1994*

♒ ◐ Samstag
20

)△♀   7:06 am
☉⚹♇   10:19 am
♇PrG   1:13 pm

© *Treelight Green 1987*

♒ ♓ ◑ Sonntag
21

)☍♂   1:15 am
)□♇   3:16 am
☉□)   4:37 am   v/c
)→♓   4:41 am
☉→♊   5:35 am
☉△♅   2:38 pm
)⚹♀   3:33 pm

Sun in Gemini 5:35 am PDT, 12:35 GMT

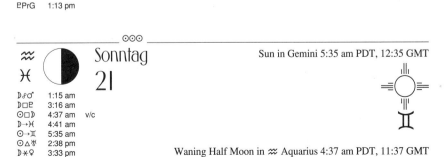

Waning Half Moon in ♒ Aquarius 4:37 am PDT, 11:37 GMT

mai

♓ lundi
22

☽□♃	2:05 am
☽□♅	2:07 pm
☽♂♄	11:18 pm

♓
♈ mardi
23

☽✶♆	3:27 am	
☽△♇	10:36 am	v/c
♂□♇	11:13 am	
☽→♈	12:14 pm	
☽✶♅	12:52 pm	
☉✶☽	4:46 pm	

♈ mercredi
24

☿sR	1:57 am
☽△♃	10:23 am
☽✶☿	11:44 pm

♈
♉ jeudi
25

♂→♍	9:10 am	
☽□♆	1:33 pm	v/c
☽→♉	10:47 pm	
☽△♂	11:19 pm	
☽□♅	11:23 pm	

♉ vendredi
26

| ☽♂♀ | 11:48 pm |

All aspects in Pacific Daylight Time; add 3 hours for EDT; add 7 hours for GMT

Moving On

□ Peni Hall 1990

Violets *Viola odorata* and *spp.*

The fifth moon beckons forth our shy woodland ally, the sweet violet, a worldwide companion to wimmin. Violet flowers and young leaves enable us to reclaim and repossess our bodies wholly, by breaking up obstructions. Violet preparations help to slowly dissolve cysts, nodules, tumors, and some cancers of the lung and breast. Teas, infusions, compresses, salves, and tinctures have

all been used for centuries. A gentle, pleasing plant of Venus, mild and cooling, violets clear heat, inflammations, blockages, and heaviness in the lungs, throat, limbs, head, liver, and psyche. Press a few fresh violets to make a meditation icon for yourself. As woodland habitats disappear, support violet survival by inviting wild violets into your garden or homescape shade areas.

© *Billie Potts 1994*

ㅕㅕㅕ

♉ samedi
27

☽⚹♄   9:59 pm

⊙⊙⊙

♉
♊   dimanche
28

☽△♆   1:38 am
☽☍♇   9:07 am   v/c
☽→♊   11:08 am
☽△♅   11:39 am
☽□♂   2:06 pm

Hestia

She proffers pen and paper,
a heartspace where words
begin: a shady grove drunk

with roses, awash in sun,
where yes or no is a paperweight
that holds a world in place.

When I enter, if I choose to enter,
I dip my pen in candleflame,
light the page with words that burn

like stars in a galaxy
that begins to speak my name.

Imagination Station   □ *Jing 1992*

VI. CREATIVITY / TRANSFORMING MOON

My Mind does deer leaps and I am Free

mayo

♊   **lunes**
29

☉☌☽   2:28 am
☽☍♃   9:11 am
☽☌☿   9:56 pm

© *Marja de Vries 1986*

New Moon in ♊ Gemini 2:28 am PDT, 9:28 GMT

♊   **martes**
30

☽ApG   12:49 am
☽□♄   11:09 am   v/c

♋   **miercoles**
31

☽→♋   12:00 am
☽✶♂   5:28 am

♋   **jueves**
1

                            # junio

☉☍♃   4:23 am
☽✶♀   3:02 pm
☽△♄   11:57 pm

♋
♌   **viernes**
2

☽☍♆   2:48 am
♀△♅   7:33 am
☽△♇   10:03 am   v/c
☽→♌   12:18 pm
☽☍♅   12:36 pm
♃PrG   4:12 pm

All aspects in Pacific Daylight Time; add 3 hours for EDT; add 7 hours for GMT

© Marja de Vries 1985

Not being able to identify my feelings
I tried to draw myself.
Only by looking at my
drawings I got to understand how
I probably felt.

ℏℏℏ

♌ ◑ sabado
3

☽△♃   8:32 am
☉✶☽   1:33 pm
☽✶☿   5:27 pm

☉☉☉

♌ ◐ domingo
♍   4

☽□♀   8:45 am
☽□♇   8:31 pm   v/c
☿PrG   9:11 pm
☉♂♉   10:39 pm
☽→♍   10:47 pm

June

♍ ## Monday
5

♐♂♂ 8:34 am
♀⚹♄ 10:29 am
☽□♃ 5:32 pm

♂♂♂

♍ ## Tuesday
6

☽□♅ 12:13 am
☉□☽ 3:27 am
♀△♆ 9:34 am
☽☍♄ 7:31 pm
☽△♆ 9:29 pm
☽△♀ 10:43 pm

☿☿☿   Waxing Half Moon in ♍ Virgo 3:27 am PDT, 10:27 GMT

♍
♎ ## Wednesday
7

☽⚹♇ 3:59 am   v/c
☽→♎ 6:14 am
☽△♅ 6:18 am
☽⚹♃ 11:18 pm

♃♃♃

♎ ## Thursday
8

☽△♅ 4:02 am
☉△☽ 1:01 pm
♅R→♑ 6:46 pm

♀♀♀

♎
♏ ## Friday
9

☽□♆ 1:50 am
♀☍♇ 7:29 am
☽□♅ 10:03 am   v/c
☽→♏ 10:04 am
☽⚹♂ 10:22 pm

All aspects in Pacific Daylight Time; add 3 hours for EDT; add 7 hours for GMT

NINE OF WANDS.
The emergence of an
obstacle which requires
ingenuity, a creative
approach.

What seems to be an untimely
setback helps even more of
our creative energy to emerge.

□ *Marj Johnston 1991*

♏	🌒	Saturday
		10

♀△♅ 8:30 am
♀→♊ 9:20 am

⊙⊙⊙

| ♏ | 🌓 | Sunday |
| ♐ | | 11 |

☽△♄ 1:39 am
☽⚹♆ 2:58 am
☽☌♇ 8:41 am
☽⚹♅ 10:44 am   v/c
☽→♐ 10:51 am
☽☍♀ 1:05 pm
⊙□♂ 3:32 pm

Juni

♐︎

Montag
12

)□♂ 12:15 am
)♂♃ 1:20 am
)♂♅ 3:42 am
)PrG 5:54 pm
☉♂) 9:05 pm

♂♂♂

Full Moon in ♐︎ Sagittarius 9:05 pm PDT
4:05 GMT

♐︎
♑︎

Dienstag
13

)□♄ 1:10 am   v/c
♂□♃ 2:26 am
)→♑︎ 10:06 am

☿☿☿

♑︎

Mittwoch
14

)△♂ 1:05 am
☿□♂ 10:50 pm

♃♃♃

♑︎
♒︎

Donnerstag
15

)✶♄ 12:48 am
)♂♆ 1:45 am
)✶♇ 7:31 am
)♂♅ 9:35 am   v/c
)→♒︎ 9:53 am
☉□♄ 4:57 pm
)△♀ 8:47 pm

♀♀♀

♒︎

Freitag
16

)✶♃ 12:06 am
)△♅ 2:02 am
☿sD 11:55 pm

All aspects in Pacific Daylight Time; add 3 hours for EDT; add 7 hours for GMT

Creation

□ *Jody Turner 1992*

Blue Vervain   *Verbena hastata*

The spiky violet-colored flowers of blue vervain glow like shimmering purple tapers above the wetlands in summer afternoons. Collected and dried carefully (with some of their top leaves), they have strong uterine and hormonal effects.*
Blue vervain flower tea supports the liver and spleen, improves circulation, and

balances hormones. An excellent, but mild fever reducer, relaxant and antispasmodic. Tincture the flowering tops in season for use in recovery from deep psychic wounds and in convalescence from debilitating illnesses. European vervain was long sacred to the Druids and Priestesses of the Mediterranean. I have found infused oil of American blue vervain a ritual ally that fires imagination and creativity, bringing forth the Muse. Hang bunches of drying flowering tops in the homespace for inspiration and protection.

*Avoid in pregnancy, but use to promote milkflow after childbirth.   © *Billie Potts 1994*

♒
♓   ☽   Samstag
             17

☉△☽   5:03 am
♀☍♃   9:09 am
☽□♇   9:37 am   v/c
☽→♓   12:14 pm

♓   ☽   Sonntag
             18

☽□♃   3:03 am
☽□♀   5:00 am
☽□♅   5:38 am
☽☍♂   8:58 am
♅♂♀   12:31 pm

Getting In Touch with the Child Within

To get in touch with my inner child I had no words so I had to do it through imagining and drawing.

Summer Solstice

© Marja de Vries 1990   **4**

© Marja de Vries 1990   **5**

© Marja de Vries 1990

6

As the light of the sun increases, we approach the time of the Summer Solstice, or Midsummer's Eve, the longest day of the year. This is a time when the sun reaches its zenith, appears to stand still for a few days, and then turns southward. It is a time to unleash the dark forces within us and to prepare for the waning of the sun's power. Native American ceremonies include a four-day fast and prayers to entreat the sun to get back on its course. In Europe, Midsummer's Eve was the strongest of the fire festivals. Fires were kept burning all night with singing, dancing, drinking of mead and ale, and love-making in the fields. One European custom at this time was to roll a burning wheel down a hillside to imitate the action of the sun and for purification of any evil spirits.

© Marcia Starck 1993, printed and excerpted from Women's Medicine Ways: Cross-Cultural Rites of Passage with permission from The Crossing Press.

juin

♓
♈
 lundi
19

DDD

☽☌♄	8:16 am	
☽✶♆	8:56 am	
☉□☽	3:02 pm	
☽△♇	3:34 pm	
☽✶♅	5:54 pm	v/c
☽→♈	6:30 pm	
☉⊼♇	10:11 pm	

▢ zana 1992

Waning Half Moon in ♓ Pisces 3:02 pm PDT, 22:02 GMT

♈ **mardi**
20

♂♂♂

☽△♃	9:59 am
☽✶☿	2:05 pm
☽✶♀	6:35 pm

♈ **mercredi**
21

☿☿☿

♀□♂	6:58 am
☉→♋	1:35 pm
☽□♆	6:21 pm

Sun in Cancer 1:35 pm PDT, 20:35 GMT

Solstice

♋

♈
♉
 jeudi
22

♃♃♃

☽□♅	3:49 am	v/c
☽→♉	4:36 am	
☉✶☽	5:54 am	

♉ **vendredi**
23

♀♀♀

| ☽△♂ | 9:26 am |

Year at a glance for CANCER ♋ (June 21–July 22)

For the last seven years, Uranus has brought unusual people into your life but kept relationships unstable, uncommitted. One of these contacts could now become something serious – especially if you share common work. As Uranus moves into Aquarius, you Cancer-born begin to explore new activities with associates, to link up with others for new and unusual purposes. Avoid becoming dependent upon anyone else's money as it will be unstable income. Inheritances or sudden windfalls are possible.

Pluto leaves your house of love and creativity in 1995. The passionate obsessiveness that you have felt in your creative projects and love affairs now focuses upon your health and your work. Jupiter joins Pluto in 1995; you may introduce techniques which add considerably to your field. Pluto tends to bring crisis wherever it goes. You may feel you have gone as far as you can in your current job and will cast about for the setting that truly suits you. Your work evolves into research, psychology, even dealing with secret or taboo subjects.

In the next few years you can completely regenerate your body if you adopt healthy habits, even if you have neglected yourself in the past. Avoid obsessive attention or fads, but do focus upon your health. Now is an excellent time for a complete physical.

With Saturn in your solar 9th house, until early 1996, your mind is serious. Your job is to gain a greater breadth of understanding, whether this occurs through academic study, travel, or philosophical inquiries. Don't think that you know everything; don't cling obsessively to a point of view. You are able to influence others through teaching, lecturing, or publishing, which heals old feelings for you of intellectual or educational inadequacy.

© Gretchen Lawlor 1994

♉
♊ ● ♄♄♄ samedi
24

)⚹♄   6:10 am
)△♆   6:24 am
)☍♇   1:40 pm
)△♅   4:04 pm   v/c
)→♊   5:03 pm

♊ ● ☉☉☉ dimanche
25

)☍♃   8:34 am
)☌♀   7:02 pm

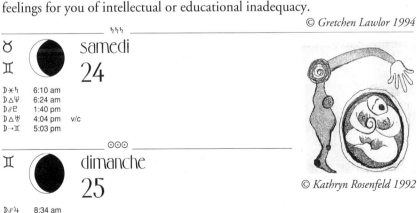

© Kathryn Rosenfeld 1992

© Nancy Bright 1988

Cradle of Love

A Sister Gone
(in memory of pat parker and all the other sisters we have lost)

a sister gone
in body but not spirit
she lingers
in our minds
our hearts
our souls
a sister gone
but not her words
they run deep
heavy in our heads
they persist fiercely on our lips
a legacy waiting to be told

a sister gone
but not her voice
the empowerment of it
rings in our ears
offering us strength to carry on
a sister gone
a sister who bestowed
the gifts of love, hope
the reaffirmation of sisterhood
a sister gone
we sisters mourn
'cause
a sister is gone

□ Laura Irene Wayne 1989

VII. SISTER / COMFORT MOON

A Healing   □ *S.J. Hugdahl 1991*

Unbound

What if feather, stone
and the bones of my dreams
unwrapped from cloth
without seams under moon
at full,
    spread down
from the door of my house,
down the stair to the street
and joined my scars,
at last laid to rest,
wrapped in cloth
without seams
under moon
on the wane

unbound from memory
I could gather seashells
and start over again.
© Ila Suzanne 1989

junio

♊

lunes
26

☽☐♂ 1:13 am
☽ApG 3:50 am
☽♂♀ 8:36 am
☽☐♄ 7:11 pm   v/c

□ *Tamara Thiebaux 1993*

♂♂♂

♊
♋

martes
27

♄⚹♆ 2:39 am
☽→♋ 5:57 am
☉♂☽ 5:51 pm

☿☿☿

New Moon in ♋ Cancer 5:51 pm PDT
00:51 GMT

♋

miercoles
28

♀☐♅ 12:49 am
☽⚹♂ 4:41 pm

♃♃♃

♋
♌

jueves
29

☽☍♆ 7:23 am
☽△♄ 7:33 am
☽△♇ 2:32 pm
☽☍♅ 4:44 pm   v/c
☽→♌ 6:03 pm

♀♀♀

♌

viernes
30

☽△♃ 8:09 am
♀☐♄ 4:09 pm

All aspects in Pacific Daylight Time; add 3 hours for EDT; add 7 hours for GMT

Recognition

Old Woman, seated near me at McDonald's,
unfashionably dressed, uncompanioned,
I recognize you!

I scan and bless the sacred hieroglyphics
graven upon your face by joy and sorrow:
the face of Mary, Isis, and Kwan Yin;
of Eve and all her daughters.
Though my arms dare not,
my soul moves to embrace you.

© Gwyneth 1993

ちちち

♌ sabado
    1

Ḏ⚹♄ 4:20 am
Ḏ⚹♀ 9:19 pm

julio

☉☉☉

♌ domingo
♍ 2

Ḏ□♇ 1:06 am v/c
Ḏ→♍ 4:36 am
Ḏ□♃ 5:50 pm

July

♍ ◑ Monday

3

☉⚹☽ 1:30 am
☿□♂ 5:45 am
☽♂♂ 6:35 pm
☽□☿ 7:18 pm

♍ ♎ ◑ Tuesday

4

☽△♆ 2:49 am
☽☍♄ 3:16 am
☽⚹♇ 9:31 am
☽△♅ 11:24 am
☽□♀ 11:50 am v/c
☽→♎ 12:56 pm
♀→♋ 11:40 pm

♎ ◐ Wednesday

5

☽⚹♃ 1:11 am
☿□♃ 1:31 am
☉□☽ 1:03 pm
♄sℝ 11:07 pm

Waxing Half Moon in ♎ Libra 1:03 pm PDT, 20:03 GMT

♎ ♏ ◑ Thursday

6

☽△☿ 7:28 am
☽□♆ 8:41 am
☽□♅ 4:44 pm v/c
☽→♏ 6:20 pm
☽△♀ 10:26 pm

♏ ◑ Friday

7

☿□♄ 12:28 am
♂♂♃ 5:30 pm
☉△☽ 8:45 pm

Healing

When I cry
Salt in my mouth
Tastes like blood licked
from a wound

□ *Sylph 1989*

All aspects in Pacific Daylight Time; add 3 hours for EDT; add 7 hours for GMT

© Tee A. Corinne 1992

We Need Every One of Us to Survive

Sisters,
Reach into the very core of your being.
Blood and bones and flesh, yes
Yet it is courage, stamina
Will and above all love
That will see us through.
All of our struggles are related
And we need every one of us to survive.

© *Sue Lorentz 1992*

ħħħ

Saturday

8

D⚹♂	8:33 am	
D⚹Ψ	11:26 am	
D△ħ	12:02 pm	
D♂P	5:29 pm	
D⚹♅	7:00 pm	v/c
D→♐	8:38 pm	

☉☉☉

Sunday

9

| D♂♃ | 7:03 am |

Juli

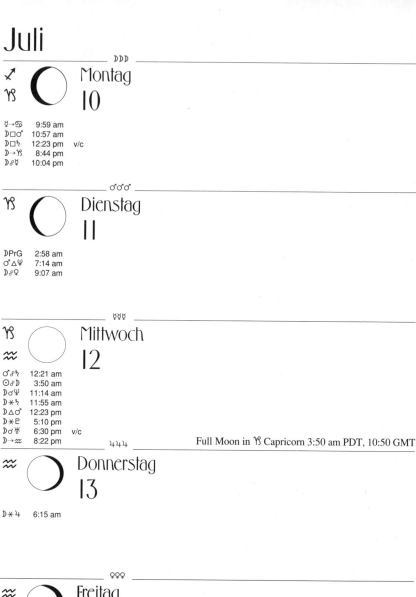

♐
♑

Montag
10

☿→♋	9:59 am
☽□♂	10:57 am
☽□♄	12:23 pm v/c
☽→♑	8:44 pm
☽☌☿	10:04 pm

♂♂♂

♑

Dienstag
11

☽PrG	2:58 am
♂△♆	7:14 am
☽☍♀	9:07 am

☿☿☿

♑
♒

Mittwoch
12

♂☍♄	12:21 am
☉☍☽	3:50 am
☽☌♆	11:14 am
☽✶♄	11:55 am
☽△♂	12:23 pm
☽✶♇	5:10 pm
☽☌♅	6:30 pm v/c
☽→♒	8:22 pm

♃♃♃

Full Moon in ♑ Capricorn 3:50 am PDT, 10:50 GMT

♒

Donnerstag
13

☽✶♃	6:15 am

♀♀♀

♒
♓

Freitag
14

☽□♇	6:13 pm v/c
☽→♓	9:38 pm

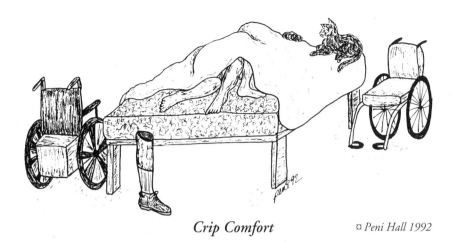

Crip Comfort   ¤ *Peni Hall 1992*

Bitter Sweet Resonance

I have been honed by pain
as the fine resonate cello
is honed by time–
and grief has kissed my face
leaving its mark upon my brow
changing forever my vision
sweetly, ever so bitter sweetly opening
my heart a little more

© *Catherine Firpo 1989*

ħħħ

♓ ☽ Samstag
15

☽□♃	7:55 am
☽△☿	1:23 pm
☉⚹♅	5:07 pm
☽△♀	8:32 pm

☉☉☉

♓ ☽ Sonntag
16

☉△☽	3:21 pm			
☽⚹♆	3:49 pm			
☽♂♄	4:42 pm			
♆PrG	7:11 pm			
☉☍♆	9:44 pm	☽△♇	10:40 pm	
☽☍♂	9:56 pm	☽⚹♅	11:59 pm	v/c

juillet

DDD

♓
♈ lundi
17

☽→♈ 2:24 am
☉△♄ 9:51 am
☽△♃ 1:18 pm
♂✳♇ 2:09 pm

¤ *Sonja Shahan 1992*

♂♂♂

♈ mardi
18

☽☐♅ 5:21 am
☽☐♀ 9:03 am
♂△♅ 5:18 pm
☽☐♆ 11:52 pm

☿☿☿

♈
♉ mercredi
19

☉☐☽ 4:11 am
☽☐♅ 8:34 am   v/c
☽→♉ 11:21 am

♃♃♃   Waning Half Moon in ♈ Aries 4:11 am PDT, 11:11 GMT

♉ jeudi
20

☿♂♀ 8:20 am
♅PrG 4:28 pm
☉△♇ 7:57 pm

♀♀♀

♉
♊ vendredi
21

♂→♎ 2:22 am
☽✳♀ 2:42 am
☽✳☿ 4:18 am
☉♂♅ 10:42 am
☽△♆ 11:20 am   ☽△♅ 8:19 pm
☽✳♄ 12:22 pm   ☉✳☽ 9:12 pm   v/c
☽♂♇ 7:09 pm   ☽→♊ 11:24 pm

All aspects in Pacific Daylight Time; add 3 hours for EDT; add 7 hours for GMT

Year at a glance for LEO ♌ (July 23–Aug. 22)

Uranus stands out in the chart for Leo in 1995 as it moves into Aquarius and opposes your Sun. Uranus' job is to disrupt and to encourage change and innovation. You are now ready to experience this in your significant partnerships: personal and professional. The part of you that is willing to act for change has become stronger than your desire to maintain and preserve what you already have. You are inspired to relate in new ways; you may choose to leave a relationship or to press for more independence and spontaneity. If you do not instigate the changes, someone close to you will do it for you. A new friend encourages your wild self, giving you a radically different view of life.

Saturn continues to transit Pisces and your solar 8th house until April 1996. Circumstances force you to respect other people's values as much as your own. Both Saturn and Pluto are pushing you to a deeper understanding of your sexual energy. Blocks to sexual expression are cleared by techniques or attitudes from other cultures.

Slow-moving Pluto joins Jupiter in Sagittarius after eleven years in Scorpio, where you were forced to rebuild your relationship with a parent, rebuild your family ties or even your home. If you have children, your relationship with them takes a sudden leap into greater depths. Power struggles with your child appear over differences in values.

Creative expression becomes a passion for Leo. Traumas experienced in childhood relating to self-esteem surface to be healed. Artistic Leos may leave an old medium forever, suddenly inspired to try something new. Your work becomes the expression of deep collective issues; your radical perspective shocks the establishment. © *Gretchen Lawlor 1994*

"Transcending Effort"
¤ *Suzanne Benton*

♄♄♄

♊ samedi 22

☽△♂ 12:30 am
☽☍♃ 11:00 am
☿⚹♅ 4:34 pm
☿☍♆ 7:32 pm

☉☉☉

♊ dimanche 23

Sun in Leo 12:31 am PDT, 7:31 GMT

☉→♌ 12:31 am
☿△♄ 1:18 am
☽ApG 1:20 pm

♌

julio

♊
♋

lunes
24

☽☽☽

☽□♄	1:08 am	v/c	
☽→♋	12:17 pm		
♀⚹♂	12:18 pm		
♀☍♆	12:40 pm		
☿△♇	3:19 pm		
♆△♂	3:44 pm	☿☍♅	8:46 pm
☽□♂	4:34 pm	♀△♄	10:27 pm

Herbs are hearty.
You can cry without disturbing them,
and when you're done
their fragrance surrounds you.

excerpt ◻ Sherri Rose-Walker 1993

♂♂♂

♋

martes
25

☿→♌	3:20 pm

☿☿☿

♋

miercoles
26

☉⚹♂	4:10 am	
☽☍♆	12:06 pm	
☽△♄	1:06 pm	
☽♂♀	5:34 pm	
☽△♇	7:55 pm	
☽☍♅	8:44 pm	v/c

♃♃♃

♋
♌

jueves
27

☽→♌	12:08 am
☽♂☿	7:00 am
☽⚹♂	7:22 am
☉♂☽	8:14 am
☿⚹♂	9:55 am
☽△♃	11:05 am
♀△♇	4:41 pm
☉♂☿	7:10 pm

New Moon in ♌ Leo 8:14 am PDT, 15:14 GMT

♀♀♀

♌

viernes
28

♀☍♅	12:06 am
♄☍♂	5:06 am
☿△♃	6:40 am
☉△♃	8:13 pm

All aspects in Pacific Daylight Time; add 3 hours for EDT; add 7 hours for GMT

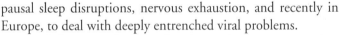

Sister Hyperica
Hypericum perforatum

Called St. Joanswort by Dianic feminist witches, St. Johnswort by Christians,
tutsan or heal-all (toutsain) by the country French. I've taken to calling this sacred
healing flower Sister Hyperica. Her

□ *Peni Hall 1992*

sunblessed flowers are the great relievers, restorers, and nurturers of flower
healing. Flower buds, open blooming flowers,* and topmost leaves are gathered
in season, infused into olive oil, or tinctured in alcohol. The deep red oil is used
for burn healing, nerve-tissue restoration, and anti-inflammatory activity,
particularly in wimmin's musculoskeletal disorders such as carpal tunnel
syndrome. Small doses of tincture are used internally for high stress, menopausal sleep disruptions, nervous exhaustion, and recently in
Europe, to deal with deeply entrenched viral problems.

Dried flowers in baths and soaks soothe soreness, sprains,
bruising, vulvitis. Hang bunches of drying flowers and top leaves
to clear tumultuous energies from the home.

*These pollen-rich flowers or tinctures can cause dermatitis or light
sensitivity in some people.

© *Billie Potts 1994*

ᒡᒡᒡ

♌
♍ sabado
29

☽□♇ 6:06 am v/c
☽→♍ 10:13 am
♀→♌ 10:33 am
☽□♃ 8:45 pm

☉☉☉

♍ domingo
30

♂⚹♃ 9:16 am

The Lesson #1

© *Megaera 1992*

VIII. WILDNESS / WILL MOON

Heart

It has to do with heart.
Her life is different because she is different.
She makes up her own mind.
Her life births a fresher start.
Old wave delusion shatters.
No more time to borrow.
No more straight line dancing.
No more angry days.
Death of the separation.
She lives, escapes suffocation.
Freedom from new age world, old world cage.
Freedom from new world order, old world lie.
Freedom from old wave delusion.
What she takes is hard to do.
What she does is hard to take.
It has to do with heart.

◻ Gentle Doe 1992

Crescent Dance   *© Julie Higgins 1993*

July

♍︎
♎︎ Monday
31

☽△♆	6:55 am	
☿ApG	7:00 am	
☽☍♄	7:45 am	
☽⚹♇	2:25 pm	
☽△♅	2:53 pm	v/c
☽→♎︎	6:24 pm	

♂♂♂

♎︎ Tuesday
1

August

☽⚹♀	12:13 am
☽⚹♃	4:33 am
☽♂♂	6:40 am
☉⚹☽	10:54 am
☽⚹☿	9:55 pm

☿☿☿

♎︎ Wednesday
2

Lammas

♃sD	9:14 am	
☽□♆	1:22 pm	
☽□♅	8:58 pm	v/c
♀△♃	10:19 pm	

♃♃♃

♎︎
♏︎ Thursday
3

☽→♏︎	12:30 am
☽□♀	11:24 am
☉□☽	8:17 pm

♀♀♀

Waxing Half Moon in ♏︎ Scorpio 8:17 pm PDT
3:17 GMT

♏︎ Friday
4

☽□☿	11:33 am
☽⚹♆	5:31 pm
☽△♄	6:09 pm

All aspects in Pacific Daylight Time; add 3 hours for EDT; add 7 hours for GMT

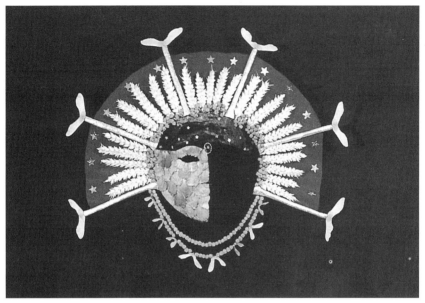

Lammas

The descent into the dark has just begun; the lushness of summer is still evident, and gardens are full of summer greens and late summer crops such as squashes, zucchini, and corn.

All cultures had representations of a corn mother or corn goddess. In Europe the corn mother was made of the last sheaves of corn harvested; her spirit was believed to be embodied in these sheaves of corn. The Mandans and Minnitareers of North America believed that a certain Old Woman Who Never Dies made the crops grow; in spring she sent various migratory birds as her representative to bring certain crops – the wild goose for maize, the wild swan for gourds, and the wild duck for beans.

It is this feeling for the corn mother, for the harvest, and for the beginnings of the cold and winter that is experienced at the time of Lammas, just as in early morning walks in August one experiences the feeling of fall in the air.

© *Marcia Starck 1993, printed and excerpted from* <u>Women's Medicine Ways:</u> <u>Cross-Cultural Rites of Passage</u> *with permission from The Crossing Press.*

Goddesszilla

godzilla –

they depict her as a
silent brainless brontosaurus
agent of destruction

watch her veridian
scaled breasts shimmer
as she harnesses fire, the
creatrix force, to destroy patriarchal
inappropriate technology, as she roars
for their attention she is a powerful
womon changing what is not to be
becoming who she is

they never show her
as she drinks in the harmony of forests
as she tends her organic garden

she is their
            worst nightmare
            their largest fear
and i tell you

SHE IS HERE

they worry the animals will get them
            back: they will!
they will restore the balance,
            reclaim their power

we are some of those animals,
wimmin,
we are some of those animals

we are restoring the balance
we are reclaiming our power

wimmin
roaring crooning
stomping dancing

join us in the changing!

goddesszilla!   ¤ *Marna Hauk 1992*

Sekmet: Lionheaded Goddess of Fire and Sun.

□ *Monica Sjöö 1991*

ħħħ

♏︎
♐︎

Saturday
5

☽♂♇	12:34 am	
☽⚹♅	12:44 am	v/c
☽→♐︎	4:15 am	
☽♂♃	1:34 pm	
☽△♀	7:28 pm	
☽⚹♂	8:07 pm	

☉☉☉

♐︎

Sunday
6

☉△☽	2:46 am	
♀⚹♂	10:12 am	
☽□♄	7:59 pm	
☽△♅	9:22 pm	v/c

August

© *Sudie Rakusin 1983*

♐ ☽☽☽
♑ 　 ## Montag
7

☽→♑　5:53 am
♅✶♇　5:58 pm
☽□♂　11:24 pm

♑ ♂♂♂
 ## Dienstag
8

♇sD　5:08 am
☽PrG　6:55 am
☿□♇　12:30 pm
☽☌♆　8:03 pm
☽✶♄　8:30 pm

♑ ☿☿☿
♒ ## Mittwoch
9

☽☌♅　2:51 am
☽✶♇　2:56 am　v/c
☽→♒　6:29 am
☽✶♃　3:35 pm
☿→♍　5:14 pm

♒ ♃♃♃
Donnerstag
10

☽△♂　2:11 am
☽☍♀　6:13 am
☉☍☽　11:17 am

Lunar Lammas
Full Moon in ♒ Aquarius 11:17 am PDT, 18:17 GMT

♒ ♀♀♀
♓ ## Freitag
11

☽□♇　4:08 am　v/c
☽→♓　7:47 am
☽☍♅　1:18 pm
☽□♃　5:20 pm

All aspects in Pacific Daylight Time; add 3 hours for EDT; add 7 hours for GMT

From The Senoi: Dream Modifiers

I will not think of death
Anymore.
I will not let those dreams
Control my days.
I will be
Mistress of my night,
My own dream maker.

I will cast off
Those bondages.
The smell of burning
Rubber will offend your nostrils
As unwanted warpings
Ignite in the heat
Of my angry skin.

I will grow labia
Enormous as sunflowers
On my head to offend.
Some rogue growths
Developing thorns
And vengeful wills
Of their own,
I will not restrain.

When thrown onto burning pyres
My sisters and I will
Ascend immediately
To paradise
To celebrate our
Glorious and well earned
Widowhood.

And our feet will
Learn to dance
Once more,
Sharp as needles
Trampling to compost
The weeping
Lotus petals.

excerpt © Berta Freistadt 1982

ℵℵℵ

♓ Samstag
12

♀□♃ 10:36 pm

☉☉☉

♓
♈ Sonntag
13

☽⚹♆ 12:05 am
☽♂♄ 12:20 am
☽⚹♅ 7:26 am
☽△♇ 7:48 am   v/c
☽→♈ 11:42 am
☽△♃ 10:02 pm

août

DDD
♈ lundi

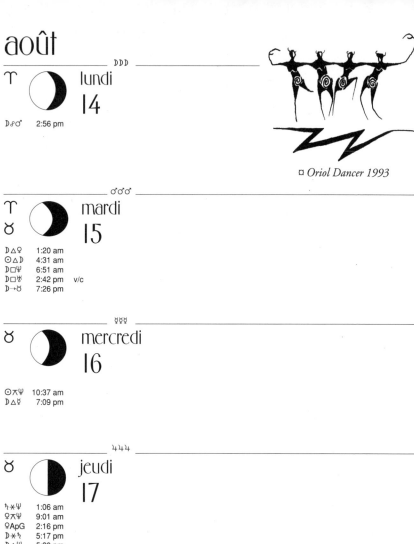

14

D☌♂ 2:56 pm

¤ *Oriol Dancer 1993*

♂♂♂
♈
♉ mardi

15

D△♀ 1:20 am
☉△D 4:31 am
D□♆ 6:51 am
D□♅ 2:42 pm v/c
D→♉ 7:26 pm

☿☿☿
♉ mercredi

16

☉⊼♆ 10:37 am
D△☿ 7:09 pm

♄♄♄
♉ jeudi

17

♄✶♆ 1:06 am
♀⊼♆ 9:01 am
♀ApG 2:16 pm
D✶♄ 5:17 pm
D△♆ 5:20 pm
D□♀ 6:19 pm
☉□D 8:05 pm

Waning Half Moon in ♉ Taurus 8:05 pm PDT
3:05 GMT

♀♀♀
♉
♊ vendredi

18

D△♅ 1:32 am
D☍♇ 2:20 am v/c
D→♊ 6:41 am
D☍♃ 6:40 pm

All aspects in Pacific Daylight Time; add 3 hours for EDT; add 7 hours for GMT

© Nancy Ann Jones 1993

Jamaica/Hibiscus *Hibiscus rosa sinensis spp.*

All across the Caribbean and Central America, in the high heat of summer, hibiscus flower tea cools excess fire, replenishing electrolytes, minerals, and flavonoids. The clear, red brews enliven us through summer heaviness, diminish torpor, restore energy, spur achievement, balance us, and strengthen will and creative powers. A great soother internally and externally like its mallow family relations, hibiscus flower keeps our bodies open and energies flowing. Teas and infusions loosen mucus and congestion, and calm irritated mucosal membranes of throat, lungs, and intestines. Hibiscus works exceptionally well with the loosening, dispersing action of honey, making it a

 wonderful partner flower for children, the very old, and those weakened by long illnesses. Its scintillating color and spiky tartness provide celebratory drinks that beneficially replace beer and sangria. It has a long flowering season; just keep plucking and drying on screens. It can be grown in large containers in northerly climates. © *Billie Potts 1994*

♄♄♄

♊ samedi
19

☽□♅ 4:41 pm
☽△♂ 7:32 pm

○○○

♊
♋   dimanche
20

☽ApG 4:42 am
☽□♄ 5:35 am
☽⚹♀ 2:01 pm
☉⚹☽ 2:06 pm   v/c
☉♂♀ 5:05 pm
☽→♋ 7:25 pm

agosto

♋ **lunes**
21

♀□♇ 12:16 am
☉□♇ 2:19 am
♅△♂ 6:21 am

♋ **martes**
22

☽□♂ 11:19 am
☽⚹♅ 1:53 pm
☽△♄ 5:27 pm
♀→♍ 5:44 pm
☽☍♆ 5:56 pm

♋
♌ **miercoles**
23

Sun in Virgo 7:36 am PDT, 14:36 GMT

☽☍♅ 1:53 am
☽△♇ 3:03 am v/c
☽→♌ 7:14 am
☉→♍ 7:36 am
☿☍♄ 6:00 pm
☽△♃ 7:22 pm
☿△♆ 10:44 pm

♍

♌ **jueves**
24

♌
♍ **viernes**
25

☽⚹♂ 12:52 am
♇⚹♄ 9:31 am
☽□♇ 12:54 pm v/c
☽→♍ 4:51 pm
☉☌☽ 9:32 pm

New Moon in ♍ Virgo 9:32 pm PDT, 4:32 GMT (August 26)

All aspects in Pacific Daylight Time; add 3 hours for EDT; add 7 hours for GMT

Year at a glance for VIRGO ♍ (Aug. 23–Sept. 22)

Saturn's shift to Pisces in 1994 brought Virgo out of fourteen years of important inner development into the social arena. This opposition to your sun lasts until 1996; challenges to the validity of this inner work are presented through your one-to-one connections. Relationships feel limiting; you are likely to detach yourself for a time to reassess whether you want to continue. If you feel drained by someone's company, you need to clarify your boundaries with them. Contacts with those who share your goals or ambitions are the most satisfying and creative.

Uranus shifts from your 5th to 6th house, signalling the end of seven years of unsettled circumstances in matters of love, children, and creativity. Change and disruption now enter your work environment and your health. Here you can be innovative and experimental, acquiring new skills, adopting new dietary or exercise regimes. Here you also tend to feel ruthless and restless. Emotional problems and psychological distress will manifest in physical symptoms.

Pluto moves from Scorpio in your 3rd house to Sagittarius in your 4th house (joined by Jupiter for 1995). Pluto's influence at the base of your chart is slow and potent – encouraging you to break away from inherited attitudes, to clean house on a physical, mental, and spiritual level. Pluto brings situations into your life that are replays of earlier traumas and difficulties. It's all being brought into the open for clearing. Jupiter speeds up the action in 1995. You could make progress, but don't push too much or too fast.

Chiron spends the first nine months of 1995 in your sign, accentuating the healing nature of this time. Old self-wounding habits can be overcome. Though you are becoming more sociable, you still need time for occasional replenishing solitude.

© *Gretchen Lawlor 1994*

"*Amazon Warrior*"
© *Megaera 1991*

♍ ● ♄♄♄ sabado
26

☽♂♀	12:29 am
☽□♃	4:49 am
☿△♅	5:14 pm

♍ ◗ ☉☉☉ domingo
27

☿⚹♇	6:12 am			
☿♂♆	10:48 am			
☽☍♄	10:56 am			
☽△♆	11:48 am			
♂□♆	12:36 pm			
☽△♅	7:04 pm	☽♂♀	10:08 pm	v/c
☽⚹♇	8:29 pm	♀□♃	11:53 pm	

They Didn't Get Me

They told us in school one
time that a beautiful creek
ran down Dolores St. and that on
Noe St. Indians fished for their supper, we were told–
      Can't you just see cornfields
spreading all over the Mission?
And all that time,
the earth wasn't confined
to backyards and fences and the 'country'–
      the weeds kept telling
me something I couldn't hear–
the earth was laughing and listening and singing
all that time. All our destruction
can't touch it. It lies in wait.

They can't touch us.
They didn't get us.   *exerpt ¤ Alma Luz Villanueva 1993*

*as a deer ♀ i survive due to the grace of
she who weaves the cycles of wholeness*

¤ Oriol Dancer 1993

IX. EARTH AS SURVIVOR MOON

This Mother Ain't For Sale

August

♍
♎ Monday
28

☽→♎ 12:16 am
☽✶♃ 12:07 pm
☿→♎ 7:08 pm

♎ Tuesday
29

☽□♆ 5:42 pm
☽☌♂ 8:27 pm

♎
♏ Wednesday
30

☽□♅ 12:43 am v/c
☽→♏ 5:52 am
☉□♃ 5:52 am
☉✶☽ 6:30 pm
☽✶♀ 11:47 pm

♏ Thursday
31

☽△♄ 8:50 pm
☽✶♆ 10:04 pm

♏
♐ Friday
1

September

☽✶♅ 4:50 am
☽☌♇ 6:30 am v/c
☽→♐ 9:58 am
☽✶♃ 6:40 pm
☽☌♃ 9:47 pm

All aspects in Pacific Daylight Time; add 3 hours for EDT; add 7 hours for GMT

Whole Cycles Regeneration Mandala

Crossing the lands of Agribusiness. Felt the contrast of the half-world of affluence and the half of drought and starvation. Felt the Harvest Mother grieving the death of her starving child, as she herself is chained and forced to overproduce for its greedy sibling. Agribusiness lands of chemical farming, giant machines, stubble burning, rolling of giant bales which can only be handled by massive machinery, massive overproduction and waste; grain mountains rot while the other half starves and dies.

© *Jill Smith 1985*

♐ Saturday 2

☉□☽	2:04 am
☽□♀	8:22 am
♂□♅	9:52 am
☽□♄	11:40 pm

Waxing Half Moon in ♐ Sagittarius 2:04 am PDT, 9:04 GMT

♐ ♑ Sunday 3

☽⚹♂	8:45 am	v/c
☿⚹♃	10:07 am	
☽→♑	12:46 pm	

September

DDD

♑ **Montag**
4

☽□☿	1:50 am
☉△☽	8:11 am
☽△♀	3:30 pm
☽PrG	6:10 pm

"Talking Rocks"
⌂ *Julia Doughty 1993*

♂♂♂

♑
≈ **Dienstag**
5

☽⚹♄	1:34 am	
☽☌♆	3:10 am	
☽☌♅	9:39 am	
☽⚹♇	11:32 am	
☽□♂	1:12 pm	v/c
☽→≈	2:48 pm	

☿☿☿

≈ **Mittwoch**
6

☽⚹♃	2:59 am
☽△☿	8:00 am

♃♃♃

≈
♓ **Donnerstag**
7

♂→♏	12:01 am	
☽□♇	1:52 pm	v/c
☽→♓	5:09 pm	
☽△♂	5:59 pm	

♀♀♀

♓ **Freitag**
8

☽□♃	6:00 am
☉☍☽	8:38 pm

Full Moon in ♓ Pisces 8:38 pm PDT, 3:38 GMT (September 9)

All aspects in Pacific Daylight Time; add 3 hours for EDT; add 7 hours for GMT

Tsagaglalal:
She Who Watches

Cascade Tsagaglalal

This prehistoric Wishram Indian legend is one of the few remaining stories about the time before patriarchy when women were still the rulers:

When Coyote came down the river he asked to meet the chief. He was taken to a woman who lived high up in the village overlooking the Columbia River. When he asked whether she was a good chief, she did not speak about wars and conquests, but that her people had good houses, much food, and were well cared for. He informed her that changes were coming and women would no longer be the chiefs. The story goes that because she was such a good chief, he turned her to stone so she could survive and watch over her people through the dark ages to come until women would again be the chiefs.

It is unclear whether Coyote was an ally (as the story implies) or a forerunner of the patriarchal takeover: a trickster who *says* he is protecting her but is really immobilizing her resistance. In any case, she is an archetypal survivor. She survives the abuses of patriarchy in the way many women have: by turning to stone. This is the trickster of the survivor strategy: by not being there in her body, in her feelings, in the present, in her vitality, she is able to endure what is otherwise unendurable.

Tsagaglalal can still be seen watching over the Columbia River basin. She is on the Washington side, looking over into Oregon near Carson Hotsprings. Most of the surrounding sacred sites are now under water due to damming of the river.

▢ *adapted by Musawa 1994*

ㅅㅅㅅ

♓
♈ 🌑 Samstag

9

♀☍♄ 6:14 am
☽☌♄ 6:38 am
☽☍♀ 6:40 am
☽✶♅ 8:46 am
♄→♎ 9:48 am
☽✶♅ 3:35 pm

☽△♇ 5:53 pm   v/c
☽→♈ 9:15 pm

☉☉☉

♈ 🌑 Sonntag

10

♀△♉ 5:34 am
☽△♃ 11:12 am

septembre

□ *Sonja Shahan 1992*

♈ 🌘 **lundi**
11

☽☍☿ 12:03 am
☽□♆ 3:03 pm
☽□♅ 10:16 pm v/c

♂♂♂

♈
♉ 🌘 **mardi**
12

☽→♉ 4:22 am
☽☍♂ 11:17 am

☿☿☿

♉ 🌗 **mercredi**
13

♀△♅ 7:06 am
☉△☽ 8:43 pm
☽⚹♄ 9:43 pm

♃♃♃

♉
♊ 🌓 **jeudi**
14

☽△♆ 12:43 am
☽△♅ 8:18 am
☉☍♄ 8:20 am
♄PrG 10:06 am
☽△♀ 11:14 am
☽☍♇ 11:14 am v/c
♀⚹♇ 11:15 am
☽→♊ 2:49 pm

♀♀♀

♊ 🌓 **vendredi**
15

☽☍♃ 7:30 am
♀→♎ 10:02 pm
☉△♆ 10:06 pm

All aspects in Pacific Daylight Time; add 3 hours for EDT; add 7 hours for GMT

photo by Joyce Meyers

□ Oriol Dancer 1993

Red Clover Blossoms   *Trifolium pratense*

The early flowers of red clover gift us all with nutritive treasures, flavonoids and minerals, estrogen analogs, anti-clotting agents, and antispasmodic compounds. She is also a wondrous earth restorer, replenishing nitrogen and minerals to depleted soils. Red clover flowers have a long herstory as a system cleanser, rebuilder, and anticancer remedy. Infusions are effective in relieving bronchitis and other spasmodic/wracking respiratory difficulties, lymphatic

swellings, and some types of arthritis. A mild, nourishing, non-disruptive blossom friend. Gather frequently in the beginning of its bloom time and dry successive batches on screens. Prepare tinctures, tisanes, syrups, and salves for winter use. Red clover is another excellent companion flower for the very young, the elderly, and those recovering from debilitating conditions. Excellent seed is now available for planetary replenishment.

© *Billie Potts 1994*

ካካካ

♊ samedi
16

☽△♅   3:58 am
☽□♄   9:26 am
☉□☽   2:10 pm   v/c
♀♂♆   6:30 pm
☽ApG   11:09 pm

Waning Half Moon in ♊ Gemini 2:10 pm, 21:10 GMT

☉☉☉

♊
♋ dimanche
17

☽→♋   3:17 am
☽□♀   6:42 am
☽△♂   5:45 pm

---

septiembre

 lunes
18

♋

D□♥ 6:46 pm
D△♄ 9:29 pm

♂♂♂

  martes
19

♋
♌

D☍♆ 1:10 am
☉⚹D 7:49 am
D☍♅ 8:43 am
D△♇ 12:00 pm v/c
D→♌ 3:20 pm
☉△♅ 6:45 pm

☿☿☿

♌ miercoles
20

D⚹♀ 1:27 am
D□♂ 8:51 am
D△♃ 8:54 am

♃♃♃

♌ jueves
21

D⚹♅ 6:25 am
☉⚹♇ 12:53 pm
D□♇ 9:58 pm v/c

♀♀♀

♌
♍ viernes
22

D→♍ 1:02 am
♥sR 2:09 am
D□♃ 6:19 pm
D⚹♂ 8:48 pm

All aspects in Pacific Daylight Time; add 3 hours for EDT; add 7 hours for GMT

Year at a glance for LIBRA ♎ (Sept. 23–Oct. 22)

In 1995, Libra hovers on the edge of a more public and influential life. For a normally sociable sign, during the last twelve to fourteen years your primary focus has been upon inner development. Soon your sphere of influence will expand; by 1996 you will be more in the public eye. 1995 is a year of housecleaning and preparation for this debut. Organize yourself: refine your skills, develop new techniques, and eliminate unnecessary involvements.

Health problems that occur this year are indicators of toxic overload. Your body needs to eliminate; dietary and exercise regimes support this. If you are experiencing total burnout, it's a sign that you have diverged from your true path somewhere. Chiron's position later in the year indicates the possibility of a healing crisis – a withdrawal from your current life situation that will help you to reorient yourself. It will be followed by renewed vitality and clarity.

Uranus, your genius self, will be in your house of creativity for the next seven years. Be willing to experiment with unusual hobbies or recreations. You uncover a zany flair and the world loves your unique approach. Contacts with children will keep you on your toes. With Jupiter's influence you could take classes to explore this creative burst, or even teach them. Uranus also influences your love life. Existing relationships need to change, become less predictable, more fun. An affair may catalyze your emotional or sexual life; don't expect it to be enduring.

Pluto begins a slow transit of your 3rd house; you hunger for more significant interactions in your daily contacts. Communications with a sibling or neighbor push you to reconsider your attitudes. Writing may become an important outlet for erupting feelings.   © *Gretchen Lawlor 1994*

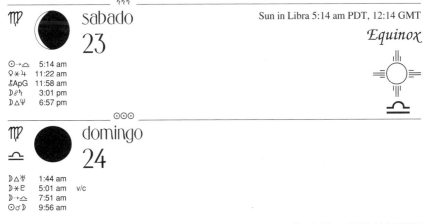

ħħħ

♍ sabado
23

☉→♎	5:14 am
♀⚹♃	11:22 am
⚷ApG	11:58 am
☽☍♄	3:01 pm
☽△♆	6:57 pm

Sun in Libra 5:14 am PDT, 12:14 GMT

Equinox

♎

☉☉☉

♍
♎ domingo
24

☽△♅	1:44 am	
☽⚹♇	5:01 am	v/c
☽→♎	7:51 am	
☉☌☽	9:56 am	

New Moon in ♎ Libra 9:56 am PDT, 16:56 GMT

Restoring The Balance: Drawing Parallels

The Earth and many other survivors are breaking their silences. This is stopping the cycle of abuse. Survivors are confronting their perpetrators. The Earth is ending the deadly cycle of abuse that she has been surviving for the last few thousand years. She is breaking her silence, screaming: "I'm not going to take any more of your abuse! Enough is enough!" One way she breaks her silence is through her Earth "changes," through increasing frequency of earthquakes, fire, flood, erosion, and drought.

This is a time of restoring balance. Breaking the silence is one way to do this. Most of the time, this restoration to balance is not well received. For example, when a survivor breaks her silence, those confronted usually perceive this act as damaging to themselves. Similarly, those affected by the Earth breaking her silence, through "natural disaster," only perceive how damaging it is to themselves and their lives. They do not see a survivor confronting abuse. In both cases balance is being restored. The *real damage* was perpetrated against the survivor, whether she be human or the Earth. This abuse is rampant and socially sanctioned, so it is not widely *recognized*. Sexism and violence against womyn and children are at the foundation of patriarchal culture. So when abuse and violence happen, it blends into the background. Similarly, those living in a way that is societally normal (by Western standards) do not perceive their lifestyle as damaging to this planet; it is expected that the Earth should be *used up* at an outrageous and unsustainable rate. This is not even questioned by most people. Human lifestyle *is* raping the Earth. She is saying "No!"; she is fighting back. We are saying "No!"; we are fighting back. We are breaking our silences; we are restoring the balance. This is critical to our survival and the survival of the planet. Blessed be.

© Beth Freewomon 1994

© Red Raven 1993

Fall Equinox

This time of equal day and equal night is a time to gather the harvest and reap what we have sown in the spring. The abundance of the harvest is present, but so is our sense of preparation for the dark, cold winter and the death of nature. Fall Equinox is the time Demeter mourns for Persphone and thus causes all in the natural world to die and mourn with her. In other goddess cultures, Astarte mourned Adonis (Syria), Cybele mourned Attis (Phrygia), and Isis mourned Osiris (Egypt). It is a time of going within ourselves and making preparations for our survival, physically and spiritually, during the winter months. In terms of directions, fall is west, the home of the black bear, the time for introspection and deep thought.

© Marcia Starck 1993, printed and excerpted from <u>Women's Medicine Ways:</u> <u>Cross-Cultural Rites of Passage</u> with permission from The Crossing Press.

□ *Becca Butcher Schoenfliess 1993*

Ginkgo/Gingko (*Ginkgo biloba*) is the sole survivor of the oldest known tree genus *Ginkgoaceae.* This tree has survived for over 400 million years. A native of China, it grows well in Oregon and other states. Ginkgo is such a survivor she is being planted in highly polluted areas as an air purifier. Used as a brain tonic for centuries, Ginkgo helps survivors with emotional stability, memory function, alertness, and increased energy. Use consistently for three months.

□ *Annie Ocean 1994*

My Toolbox
(℞ to Prevent Relapse)

As I meander up from the Abyss
I carry my toolbox with me.

It is small and compact enough
to nestle in my pocket like keys
or hang from a sturdy thong
cradled between my breasts.

It is curved and leathery smooth
like the earthy shell of a turtle.
Its geodesic strength can withstand
even the misstep of my elephant days.

In this tiny box is a bell,
its pure tone alert to the approach
of the heavy-limbed times.
This tone reminds me to fill
fifteen moments with the activity of
picking up the pieces of my life
one by one.

Also in this box is the wind,
free for the catching.
I'm here only to let it flow peacefully
into the deepest, softest part of my being.
It floats softly like warm downy fluff
and softens the thistles of my mouth
and my piercing, inner shoulds.

And in this precious box,
is one clear drop of water.
The patient steady trickle
of cleansing affirmations
smoothes the ancient jagged bedrock
and turns muddy waters clear.

Finally, there is a window within this box
to let the quickening spark be seen.
Joined with other precious flames,
we'll warm the world around.
As I draw my map each day,
this blaze will illuminate the rising path.

With these tools I continue.
I rise up out of the shadowy chasm
and I step into today.   ◻ *Pam EH! 1993*

Amazon Angel © *Megaera 1991*

Declaration of Self

I am a woman flanked by lionstrength, and
angels circle hawklike above my head.
I am a woman
holding my ground against
a hurricane of patriarchal opposition, but I am
only one of many sisters: We will reclaim our Earth, our Selves, our Goddess.
I am independent, but accept help when it is needed
without guilt, without shame, without a feeling of indebtedness.
I am loved.

excerpt © Diana Rose Hartwoman 1993

September

♌♌♌

♎ Monday
25

☽✶♃	12:53 am
☽☌♀	4:13 am
☉☌♴	2:43 pm
☽☌♅	6:02 pm
☽□♆	11:54 pm

♂♂♂

♎
♏ Tuesday
26

| ☽□♅ | 6:26 am | v/c |
| ☽→♏ | 12:21 pm | |

☿☿☿

♏ Wednesday
27

| ☽☌♂ | 12:01 pm |
| ☽△♄ | 11:05 pm |

♃♃♃

♏
♐ Thursday
28

☽✶♆	3:17 am	
☽✶♅	9:41 am	
☽☌♇	1:02 pm	v/c
☽→♐	3:31 pm	

♀♀♀

♐ Friday
29

☉✶☽	1:12 am
☽☌♃	8:51 am
☿☌♀	12:41 pm
☽✶♅	7:41 pm
☽PrG	8:41 pm
☽✶♀	8:50 pm

All aspects in Pacific Daylight Time; add 3 hours for EDT; add 7 hours for GMT

¤ *Tamara Thiebaux 1993*

♐
♑

Saturday
30

☽□♄ 1:34 am v/c
☽→♑ 6:11 pm

♑

Sunday
1

October

☉□☽ 7:37 am
☽□♀ 7:02 pm
☽⚹♂ 10:44 pm

Waxing Half Moon in ♑ Capricorn 7:37 am PDT, 14:37 GMT

Oktober

"New Bloom"
© *Judith Burros 1990*

♑
♒

Montag
2

☿☊♄ 12:12 am
☽⚹♄ 4:01 am
☽□♀ 4:24 am
☽☌♆ 8:43 am
☽☌♅ 3:06 pm
☽⚹♇ 6:42 pm v/c
☿PrG 7:32 pm
☽→♒ 9:00 pm

♒

Dienstag
3

☉△☽ 2:25 pm
☽⚹♃ 3:40 pm
☽△☿ 6:21 pm

♒

Mittwoch
4

☽□♂ 4:35 am
♀□♆ 5:27 am
☉⚹♃ 11:19 am
☽△♀ 12:43 pm
♆sD 5:14 pm
☉☌☿ 6:18 pm
☽□♇ 10:22 pm v/c
☿⚹♃ 10:40 pm

♒
♓

Donnerstag
5

☽→♓ 12:36 am
☽□♃ 8:20 pm

♓

Freitag
6

♂△♄ 1:12 am
♅sD 3:16 am
☽☌♄ 11:16 am
☽△♂ 11:52 am
☽⚹♆ 4:44 pm
☽⚹♅ 11:27 pm

All aspects in Pacific Daylight Time; add 3 hours for EDT; add 7 hours for GMT

Letting Light In

Sometimes healing
      needs no words
  but happens
      one small moment
    at a time
    around the edges

like stars
     on a spring night
each one
    bringing its small gift
      of light
      and hope
    enough to bear
      us Home
    across the Twilight.

© *Lois Bresee 1990*

¤ *Jody Turner 1992*

ħħħ

♓
♈   Samstag
    7

☽△♇   3:30 am   v/c
☽→♈   5:43 am
♀□♅   5:49 am
☽☍♉   8:15 pm

☉☉☉

♈   Sonntag
    ♉

☽△♃   2:55 am
☉☍☽   8:53 am
☽□♆   11:32 pm

Appulse Lunar Eclipse 9:04 am PDT (.825 magn.)
Full Moon in ♈ Aries 8:53 am PDT, 15:53 GMT

octobre

♈ ♉ **lundi**

9

☽□♅ 6:33 am
☽☍♀ 11:50 am v/c
☽→♉ 1:06 pm

"Crip Fantasy - Tool for the Job"
☐ *Peni Hall 1992*

♂♂♂

♉ **mardi**

10

♀→♏ 12:49 am
♂⚹♆ 9:43 am

☿☿☿

♉ ♊ **mercredi**

11

☽⚹♄ 2:22 am
☽△♆ 8:59 am
☽☍♂ 10:23 am
☽△♅ 4:21 pm
☽☍♇ 9:03 pm v/c
☽→♊ 11:11 pm

♃♃♃

♊ **jeudi**

12

☽△☿ 9:25 am

♀♀♀

♊ **vendredi**

13

☽☍♃ 12:03 am
☽□♄ 1:39 pm
☉△☽ 3:21 pm v/c
☿sD 5:42 pm
☿♂⚷ 7:19 pm

All aspects in Pacific Daylight Time; add 3 hours for EDT; add 7 hours for GMT

Broken Hearted Butch Madonna Mends Her Own Heart

© Sierra Lonepine Briano 1991

♄♄♄

♊
♋

samedi
14

☽→♋ 11:21 am
☽△♇G 6:57 pm
☽□♉ 9:42 pm
☽△♀ 11:50 pm

☉☉☉

♋

dimanche
15

♉☌♃ 2:18 am
♂⚹♅ 6:17 pm

octubre

♋
♌

lunes
16

☽△♄	1:57 am
☉□♇	8:58 am
☽☍♆	9:25 am
☉□☽	9:27 am
☽☍♅	4:57 pm
☽△♂	6:21 pm
☽△♇	9:59 pm v/c
☽→♌	11:47 pm

Waning Half Moon in ♋ Cancer 9:27 am PDT, 16:27 GMT

♌

martes
17

☽⚹♅	12:10 pm
☽□♀	6:53 pm

♌

miercoles
18

☽△♃	2:14 am

♌
♍

jueves
19

☉⚹☽	1:37 am
☽□♂	8:32 am
☽□♇	8:39 am v/c
☽→♍	10:12 am
♂☌♇	10:29 am

♍

viernes
20

☉□♅	4:46 am
☽⚹♀	10:24 am
☽□♃	12:03 pm
♂→♐	2:03 pm
☽☍♄	9:12 pm

All aspects in Pacific Daylight Time; add 3 hours for EDT; add 7 hours for GMT

Breathing Through Fear

¤ *Debby Earthdaughter 1993*

Yerba Santa   *Eriodictyon californica*

Hiking in the chaparral in the bloom time of yerba santa, when it has a sweet, spicy aroma, stimulates our higher centers and affirms body and spirit. The luminous lavender flowering tops and uppermost leaves provide healing support in all types of respiratory difficulties: asthma, bronchitis, chest and head colds, coughs, throat soreness, and lung and sinus congestions. Chewing  a bit of flower and leaf energizes without overstimulating. Using small amounts of tea or tincture in ten-to-fourteen-day courses strengthens oxygenation capability. The flowers are opening and clearing in steams and sweats. Hanging the flowering tops to dry in the living space purifies the air and disperses healing energy throughout the home. Encourage dry country and chaparral dwellers to landscape their land with yerba santa.

© *Billie Potts 1994*

ħħħ

♍
♎   🌑   sabado
21

☽△♆	4:28 am	
☽△♅	11:15 am	
☽⚹♇	3:57 pm	v/c
☽→♎	5:16 pm	
☽⚹♂	6:47 pm	

☉☉☉

♎   🌑   domingo
22

| ☽♂♉ | 12:42 pm |
| ☽⚹♃ | 6:16 pm |

Memories from Hel

They say the Goddesses of Hel
Hold unwanted children
And it's true and they held me
Till I knew I was loved

It doesn't surprise any of us
That it was the earth who received us
When no one else would
And took us into the dark

I've never been afraid
of the dark, it always seemed the sun
Was harsh, exposing, critical
While everyone looks the same
When the lights go out

You can hide there,
You can disappear,
Bury your face and suck dirt
Into your nostrils
Until you die the sweet
slow death of Holda

Now when people ask me
Why I turn to the Banshee
For the source of my freedom,
Why is it the wail of
Death that liberates me

Then it is, of course,
That her howl wakes me
Reminds me of Hel
The only place I was ever
Loved

XI. MASKS / FACING FEARS MOON

¤ *Megan Wilson 1993*

October

♎︎
♏︎

Monday
23

☽□♆	9:02 am	
☉→♏︎	2:33 pm	
☽□♅	3:28 pm	v/c
☽→♏︎	9:07 pm	
☉☌☽	9:37 pm	

Sun in Scorpio 2:33 pm PDT, 21:33 GMT

♏︎

Lunar Samhain
Total Solar Eclipse (2 min. 10 sec.) 9:32 pm PDT
New Moon in ♏︎ Scorpio 9:37 pm PDT
4:37 GMT

♏︎

Tuesday
24

♏︎
♐︎

Wednesday
25

♀△♄	12:19 am	
☽△♄	4:13 am	
☽☌♀	4:36 am	
☿⚹♃	7:45 am	
☽⚹♆	11:15 am	
☽⚹♅	5:30 pm	
☽☌♇	9:59 pm	v/c
☽→♐︎	10:57 pm	

♐︎

Thursday
26

☽☌♂	5:37 am	
☽PrG	2:12 pm	
☽☌♃	11:43 pm	

♐︎

Friday
27

☽⚹♀	3:33 am	
☽□♄	5:24 am	v/c

All aspects, except Oct. 29, in Pacific Daylight Time; add 3 hours for EDT; add 7 hours for GMT

Year at a glance for SCORPIO ♏ (Oct. 23–Nov. 21)

Finally, after eleven intense years, Pluto moves out of Scorpio and into Sagittarius on January 16, 1995. It retrogrades into Scorpio during late May for six months, but its influence is diluted by the contact with Sagittarius. The pressure in your life should begin to lessen. Years of crisis and intensity have left you with a supreme ability to weather storms.

Uranus also changes sign in 1995 – from Capricorn into Aquarius – and activates the roots of your chart. You need to create a safe space for yourself. You will change your house around, redecorate or remodel, add family members, or even move to a new location. You are discovering an inner independence that has been missing in your life. A relationship with a parent changes as they change, freeing you from unconscious restrictive habits.

Stability comes from Saturn in your house of creativity. Work with art, sport, or children makes you feel you are contributing to society. It may pay the bills as well. You have a more disciplined approach to creative activities, though you may have to work harder to produce.

Pluto joins Jupiter in Sagittarius to influence your values, especially your attitude towards money. Pluto's position implies a gradual transformation over the next twelve years, bringing you greater appreciation of deeper values than those based on material acquisition. Pluto does its work through crisis; you may experience loss of material resources. This keeps you fearful and anxious, until you turn to the strength that comes from intangible sources of wealth. In 1995 Jupiter helps through your philosophy or politics. However, it may imply extravagant material outlays – best avoided, as Pluto will make you pay later through crisis. The whole world is being forced to shift from material to spiritual values; your lessons may be particularly obvious.

© Gretchen Lawlor 1994

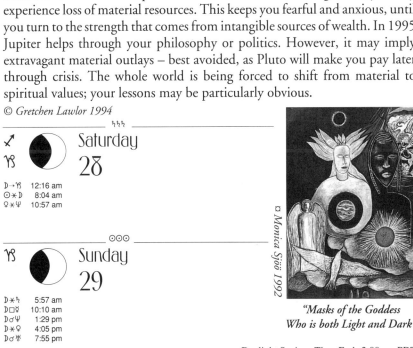

ħħħ

♐
♑

Saturday
28

☽→♑	12:16 am
☉✳☽	8:04 am
♀✳♆	10:57 am

◎◎◎

♑

Sunday
29

☽✳ħ	5:57 am
☽□♅	10:10 am
☽☌♆	1:29 pm
☽✳♀	4:05 pm
☽☌♅	7:55 pm

□ *Monica Sjöö 1992*

*"Masks of the Goddess
Who is both Light and Dark"*

Daylight Savings Time Ends 2:00 am PDT

Oktober

☽☽☽

Montag
30

© *Deborah Winter 1992*

☽✶♇ 12:40 am v/c
☽→♒ 1:24 am
☉□☽ 1:18 pm
☽✶♂ 1:44 pm
☿□♆ 4:22 pm
♂✶♄ 5:31 pm

♂♂♂

Waxing Half Moon in ♒ Aquarius 1:18 pm PST, 21:18 GMT

♒

Dienstag
31

Samhain

☽✶♃ 4:42 am
♀✶♅ 12:34 pm
☽△☿ 8:11 pm

☿☿☿

♒
♓

Mittwoch
1

November

☽□♀ 12:47 am
☽□♇ 4:41 am v/c
☽→♓ 5:18 am
☽□♂ 9:08 pm
☉△☽ 9:53 pm

♃♃♃

♓

Donnerstag
2

☿□♅ 2:09 am
☽□♃ 10:32 am
☽♂♄ 2:02 pm
♀♂♇ 8:39 pm
☽✶♆ 10:34 pm

♀♀♀

♓
♈

Freitag
3

♀→♐ 2:19 am
☽✶♅ 5:36 am
☽△♇ 10:52 am v/c
☽→♈ 11:22 am
☽△♀ 12:19 pm

All aspects in Pacific Standard Time; add 3 hours for EST; add 8 hours for GMT

Two Faced © Genece Klein 1990

Samhain/Hallowmas/All Hallows Eve are names for the celebration

that marks the end of the year and the beginning of the new cycle. This is a time when the veil between the living and dead is very thin; it is a time when we can communicate with the spirits of the ancestors and the recently departed. It is the time of transition from autumn to winter, when the spirits of the departed come back, seeking their warm homes for the next season.

Hallowe'en is the time of the crone, the wise woman, and the honoring of the crone goddesses from many cultures. These goddesses include Hecate (Greece), Kali (India), Cerridwyn (Wales), Oya (Africa), Inanna and Ereshkigal (Sumer), Nepthys (Egypt), Sedna (Inuit), Copper Woman and Spider Grandmother (Native American), Baba Yaga (Russia), the Morrigan (Ireland), Hella (Scandinavia), and Holla (Germany). The cauldron of the crone is usually used in the center of the circle for rituals. The cauldron comes from the legend of Cerridwyn who had a magic cauldron.

Many animal spirits are present at this time and speak through the witches or wise women. The custom of wearing costumes arose so mortals could impersonate these animal spirits and the spirits of the dead to bring them back to life. Many cultures invoke the spirits of departed ancestors at Hallowe'en; in Mexico this time is referred to as "El Dia de las Muertes" (the Day of the Dead) and ceremonies last a whole week. The ceremony is dedicated to the Aztec goddess Tonantzin, who later was worshipped as the Virgin of Guadalupe. The Christian world celebrates at this time and calls it All Saints' Day.

Hallows is a good time for looking into the future through the use of scrying and crystal balls; it is also an important time for getting rid of old habits and patterns. The fire in the cauldron should be used for burning and banishing the old. Prayers are also made for departed ones, for ancestors, and those we want to remember as the many wise women who were burned in Europe as witches.

No one can vie with a witch in Red things.

When the moon is waning,
get a red flannel bag, small enough to
fit into your pockets. Pass it through
some purifying smoke and call in the
angels of protection to help you put your
fears inside the bag. After you have lit a
white candle say:

I gather my fears into my red magical bag.
I include the black stones of apprehension.
[place tiny black stones into bag]
I include the red stones of anger and dissatisfaction.
[place red stones into the bag]
I include the gray stones of the fear of the unknown.
[place gray stones into the bag]
[close them and bless them]
As the Moon wanes

Let Grandmother take them away.

Hang your little bag on a tree where nobody can get it.
Forget about the entire matter.

Fear

This feeling is very dominant in our species. In the old days of our race, when we were relatively helpless, we feared the abundant predators of the wild. Today we are no less fearful, but the causes of our fears have changed. We fear fear itself, we fear love and intimacy. We also fear the enemies of the day: men fear women, women fear men's violence. The streets are battlefields – male against female and male against male. In no other species is there such brutal, persistent violence against the females and the young. Fear is our original sin.

To live in fear and with fear all the time is crippling our spirits. Excessive fear has become our entertainment. Horror movies, violent movies, TV news – all feed our fears.

To lift fear from your heart, use the above moonspell.

Survivor

I am a child
screaming behind a mask
woven by the gods
       ¤ *Lark Hajdu 1992*

¤ *Suzanne Benton 1992*

♄♄♄

♈ 🌙 **Samstag**
4

☿→♏ 12:51 am
☽△♂ 7:07 am
☽△♃ 6:41 pm

☉☉☉

♈ 🌙 **Sonntag**
♉ **5**

☽□♆ 6:23 am
☽□♅ 1:43 pm v/c
☽→♉ 7:36 pm

---

novembre

  lundi
6

☽☍♅   2:01 am
☉☍☽   11:22 pm

Full Moon in ♉ Taurus 11:22 pm PST
7:22 GMT

♉ mardi
7

☽⚹♄   6:42 am
☽△♆   4:19 pm
☽△♅   11:58 pm

♉
♊ mercredi
8

☽☍♇   5:45 am   v/c
☽→♊   5:56 am
☽☍♀   8:05 pm

♊ jeudi
9

☽☍♂   10:41 am
☽☍♃   5:33 pm
☽□♄   6:01 pm   v/c

♊
♋ vendredi
10

♀⚹⚷   2:07 am
♇→♐   11:49 am
☉△♄   3:41 pm
☽→♋   5:58 pm
♃□♄   6:31 pm

All aspects in Pacific Standard Time; add 3 hours for EST; add 8 hours for GMT

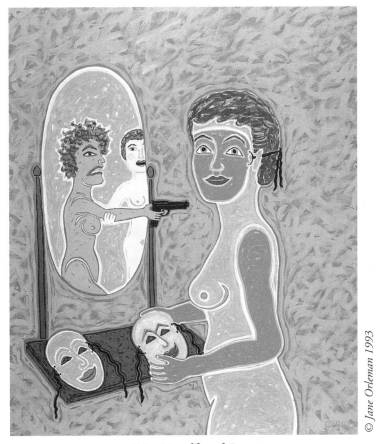

Me, Myself and I

ħħħ

 ♋ samedi
11

☽ApG   1:07 pm
☽△☿   7:41 pm

☉☉☉

 ♋ dimanche
12

☽△ħ   6:32 am
☉△☽   10:12 am
☽☌Ψ   4:54 pm

noviembre ☽☽☽

♋
♌
 lunes
13

☽☍♅ 12:51 am v/c
☽→♌ 6:38 am
☽△♇ 6:51 am

♂♂♂

♌ martes
14

♂□♄ 7:11 am
☽△♀ 10:54 am
☽□♅ 5:25 pm
☽△♂ 7:24 pm
☽△♃ 8:29 pm

☿☿☿

♌
♍
 miercoles
15

☿△♄ 2:39 am
☉□☽ 3:41 am v/c
☽→♍ 6:03 pm
☽□♇ 6:27 pm
☉⚹♆ 6:42 pm
♂♂♃ 7:45 pm

♃♃♃   Waning Half Moon in ♌ Leo 3:41 am PST, 11:41 GMT

♍ jueves
16

♀♀♀

♍ viernes
17

☽□♀ 3:16 am
☽☍♄ 4:17 am
☽□♃ 7:02 am
☽□♂ 8:34 am
☽⚹♅ 11:22 am   ☉⚹☽ 5:37 pm
♀□♄ 1:52 pm   ☽△♅ 9:23 pm v/c
☽△♆ 2:05 pm

All aspects in Pacific Standard Time; add 3 hours for EST; add 8 hours for GMT

Healer Crone

Artemisias *Artemisia spp.*

Artemisias are global, whole-healing companions of survivors and majikmakers. Mugwort, the wormwoods, sweet Annie, garden (French) tarragon, southernwood, "old man sage" (A. californica), and "sagebrush" (A. tridentata) are all sacred to moon goddesses. Artemisia flowers have an affinity with our emotional and ritual lives, whether in green stands or preserved as remedies. The grey-green or yellow-green flowers, spiky but not showy, are potent healers. Teas and tinctures of flow-

© *Megaera 1992*

ers and top leaves tone diges-
tive and reproductive organs.* Using the flowers in sweats or steams, or dried for pillows, brings buried dreams and memories to the surface, intensifies and colors other dreams and trances. These flowers powerfully release old trauma and open gateways. It is helpful to have guidance or group support in Artemisia dreaming. As dream pillows or moxa sticks, Artemisias can go anywhere.

*Avoid during pregnancy or breastfeeding.   © *Billie Potts 1994*

 ♍ sábado

♎ **18**

☽→♎	2:19 am
☽⚹♇	2:51 am
☿⚹♆	9:49 am

○○○

♎ domingo

19

♀☌♃	1:55 am
☽⚹♃	1:37 pm
☽⚹♀	2:33 pm
☽⚹♂	5:13 pm
☽□♆	7:24 pm
☉⚹♅	8:13 pm

Breaking The Fever

When I was young
fevers were attacked
the grown-ups would rub you
with alcohol
wrap you in wet sheets
refuse you blankets
fan you, feed you aspirin
plunge your wrists in cold water

They knew fever had to be fought
because it let children see
forbidden things
at 105 I would start to hear voices
soft and lulling
at 106 the faces would appear
swimming around me
with outstretched hands
they would gesture to me
to come and join them

I was always very happy then
floating out on the warm brink
of the world
the fever children
would in high voices
liquid like silver bells
come with us
they would say
come play, Mary
and they would show me
maple trees turning red and gold
long aisles of sunlight
and woods that glowed and trembled

My body would start to come apart
very gently like milkweed fluff
and I would begin
to rise up toward their
sweet hands
but always at the last moment
the dark heavy circles
of the grown-ups' faces
would force me back down
and their fear would pin my chest
to the mattress
like black crystal paperweights

XII. ALLIES / PROTECTORS MOON

An Angelique Moment

© Nance Paternoster 1992

They would force more aspirin on me
more ice and alcohol rubs
more wet sheets
and if that didn't work
they would lift my naked body
and plunge it into a tub of cold water
ignoring my screams

Come back
they would plead
come back
come back
and my fever would buckle
and snap like the spine
of a beautiful snake
crushed under a boot

Then the fever children
would abandon me
and I would be left in a world
of ordinary things:
light bulbs
used kleenex
hissing radiators
thermometers

I would see my mother's pale
terrified face
and my stuffed animals
and my brother's crib
and my precious fever would lie
broken in a thousand bits
with no way to put it back together
and I could never explain
how kind it had been
and how foolish we were to fear it.

© Mary Mackey 1990

November

ΔΔΔ

Monday
20

☽□♅ 2:14 am v/c
☽→♏ 6:41 am
☿⚹♅ 11:20 pm

♂♂♂

♏

Tuesday
21

♄sD 11:13 am
☽△♄ 12:31 pm
☽⚹♆ 9:18 pm

☿☿☿

♏
♐

Wednesday
22

Sun in Sagittarius 11:02 am PST, 19:02 GMT

☽⚹♅ 3:50 am
☽♂♉ 7:09 am
☉♂☽ 7:44 am v/c
☽→♐ 7:57 am
☽♂♇ 8:43 am
☉→♐ 11:02 am
♀♂♂ 1:31 pm
☿→♐ 2:47 pm

☉♂☿ 9:27 pm
☿♂♇ 10:16 pm
♇ApG 10:20 pm
☉♂♇ 10:45 pm

New Moon in ♏ Scorpio 7:44 am PST, 15:44 GMT

♃♃♃

♐

Thursday
23

☽□♄ 12:43 pm
☽PrG 3:15 pm
☽♂♃ 5:19 pm

♀♀♀

♐
♑

Friday
24

☽♂♂ 12:19 am
☽♂♀ 1:34 am v/c
☽→♑ 7:49 am

All aspects in Pacific Standard Time; add 3 hours for EST; add 8 hours for GMT

Year at a glance for SAGITTARIUS ♐ (Nov. 22–Dec. 21)

Pluto, the planet of power and transformation, enters Sagittarius on January 17, 1995. Except for a short retrograde into Scorpio from April 20 to November 9, it stays in Sagittarius until the year 2008.

How will this affect you Sagittarians? The last few years you've been closing the door on an old identity. Your life's direction is completely changing – you may even begin to look different.

You have a powerful effect upon others this year, which you may not always be aware of. Astrology, yoga, or any philosophy that is concerned with self-development through the discipline of your energy will benefit you. Positively, you exhibit powerful concentration, dedication to ideals, and depth of insight. Expressed negatively, it manifests as ruthless and stubborn power plays.

If you are not in touch with your need to change, it could feel as though the world is conspiring against you, forcing change upon you. Hidden aspects of your life come to light which you have not previously acknowledged. Compulsive or obsessive behavior may surface, especially to do with power and control.

Saturn has been in your solar 4th house since 1994, indicating reorganization of your domestic environment. This could mean anything from adding structurally to your home to taking on serious responsibilities for someone close to you. Home feels restrictive; you may decide to escape.

With Uranus moving into Aquarius and your 3rd house, old ways of thinking and speaking will fall away. New ideas come to you in intuitive flashes. Your thinking may be too radical for your friends and family. You may take many short journeys or even move – looking for a community of like-minded souls.   © *Gretchen Lawlor 1994*

ħħħ

♑ Saturday
25

☿ApG   8:51 am
☽⚹ħ   12:43 pm
☽☌♆   9:38 pm

☉☉☉

♑ ♒ Sunday
26

☽☌♅   4:20 am   v/c
☽→♒   8:16 am
☽⚹♇   9:19 am
☉⚹☽   3:15 pm
☽⚹☿   7:10 pm

"The Lesson" #2
© *Megaera 1992*

November

≈

Montag
27

♀→♐ 5:24 am
☽⚹♃ 8:52 pm

© Red Raven 1993

♂♂♂

≈
♓

Dienstag
28

☽⚹♂ 8:30 am   v/c
☽→♓ 11:00 am
☽□♇ 12:15 pm
☽⚹♀ 1:56 pm
☉□☽ 10:29 pm

☿☿☿

Waxing Half Moon in ♓ Pisces 10:29 pm PST
6:29 GMT

♓

Mittwoch
29

☽□♅ 5:16 am
☿⚹♄ 2:17 pm
☽♂♄ 7:02 pm

♃♃♃

♓
♈

Donnerstag
30

☽□♃ 2:46 am
☽⚹♆ 5:09 am
♂→♐ 5:59 am
☽⚹♅ 12:46 pm   v/c
☽→♈ 4:52 pm
☽□♂ 5:32 pm
☽△♇ 6:21 pm

♀♀♀

♈

Freitag
1

Dezember

☽□♀ 1:44 am
☉△☽ 9:44 am
☽△♅ 7:56 pm

All aspects in Pacific Standard Time; add 3 hours for EST; add 8 hours for GMT

Survivor Meets
the Bird Goddess

in child time
the raven's beak
pierces flesh
(wings beating in the dark)

in maiden time
eye of the hawk
polices flesh
(wings shivering in the dark)

in mother time
talons of memory
unprison flesh
(wings flapping the dark)

in crone time
owl's tongue
praises flesh
(wings flying in the dark)

in our time
heart of the phoenix
pleasures of the flesh
wings wings wings

◻ *Alise Ariel 1993*

◻ *Nikki Cash 1993*

Protector of the Child Spirit

♈ 🌘 Samstag
2

♄♄♄

☽△♃ 11:55 am
☽□♆ 1:32 pm
☽□♅ 9:35 pm   v/c

⊙⊙⊙

♈
♉ 🌘 Sonntag
3

☽→♉ 1:41 am
☽△♂ 6:06 am
☽△♀ 5:21 pm

decembre)))

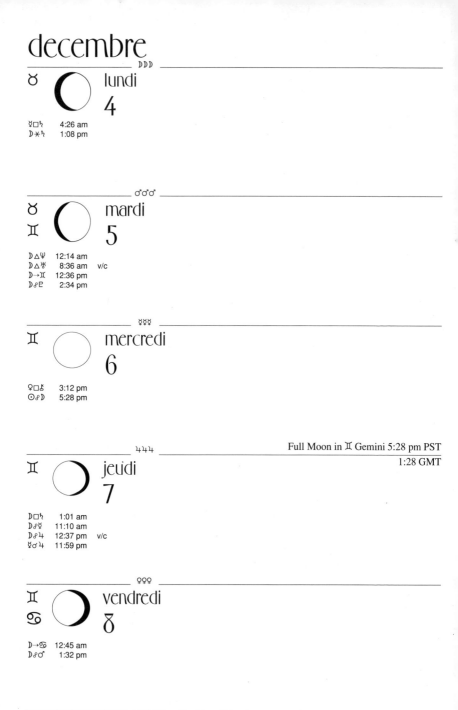

ठ **( )** lundi
4

ठ□ħ   4:26 am
)⚹ħ   1:08 pm

♂♂♂

ठ **( )** mardi
Ⅱ 5

)△Ψ   12:14 am
)△♅   8:36 am   v/c
)→Ⅱ   12:36 pm
)♂♇   2:34 pm

☿☿☿

Ⅱ **( )** mercredi
6

♀□♫   3:12 pm
☉♂)   5:28 pm

♃♃♃   Full Moon in Ⅱ Gemini 5:28 pm PST

1:28 GMT

Ⅱ **( )** jeudi
7

)□ħ   1:01 am
)♂ठ   11:10 am
)♂♃   12:37 pm   v/c
ठ♂♃   11:59 pm

♀♀♀

Ⅱ **( )** vendredi
♋ 8

)→♋   12:45 am
)♂♂   1:32 pm

All aspects in Pacific Standard Time; add 3 hours for EST; add 8 hours for GMT

Court Scene #5

A beautiful young woman with brown hair and brown eyes takes the stand.

She is calm
She is quiet
> Grandmother Owl is in her womb for protection,
> She doesn't say this.

She looks around the court room
Her vision is crisp
Her eye exact and true
> Golden Eagle is in her mind's eye for clarity
> She doesn't say this.

She fills the room with great light
And strong Ki as she breathes
> Gift of Pipe has touched her lips
> She doesn't say this.

She speaks
the Truth gently, directly
Forcefully
> The Drum, the Great Round, this Turtle Island beats true
> She doesn't say this.

After she cries.
> Ocean Spirit pours through her, Moon bathes her.
> Sisters, brothers soothe her.

She climbs to her Rock
Carrying her drum
She calls in All Relations.

She Tells All!   *□ Marie Truscott 1989*

♋ samedi
9

☽ApG   2:14 am
☽☍♀   7:02 am
☽△♄   1:44 pm

♋
♌   dimanche
10

☽☍♆   1:09 am
☽☍♅   9:51 am   v/c
☉□♄   12:48 pm
☽→♌   1:25 pm
☽△♇   3:49 pm

diciembre

 ♌ lunes
11

☿→♑ 6:58 pm

♂♂♂

♌ martes
12

♀✳♄ 12:49 am
☉△☽ 5:43 am
☽△♃ 3:51 pm   v/c

☿☿☿

♌   miercoles
♍ 13

☽→♍ 1:27 am
☽□♇ 3:59 am
☽△☿ 5:56 am
☽△♂ 9:51 pm

♃♃♃

♍   jueves
14

☽☍♄ 1:22 pm
☽△♀ 7:46 pm
☉□☽ 9:32 pm

♀♀♀

Waning Half Moon in ♍ Virgo 9:32 pm PST

5:32 GMT

♍ viernes
♎ 15

☽△♆ 12:04 am
☽□♃ 3:07 am
☽△♅ 8:19 am   v/c
☽→♎ 11:10 am
☽✳♇ 1:44 pm
☽□☿ 11:12 pm

All aspects in Pacific Standard Time; add 3 hours for EST; add 8 hours for GMT

□ *Debby Earthdaughter 1992*

Calendula* *Calendula officinalis*

The glowing orange calendula flower has been a we'moon protectress since ancient times. Infuse the flowers in the healing oils of olive or almond for soothing skin problems and preventing deep injury when there has been an accident. Tincture in alcohol for trauma-relieving liniments. Warm baths and soaks with calendula flowers bring healing to sore or tender tissues. Hot foot soaks of calendula blossoms evaporate stress, tension headaches, and relentless worry. Weak tea or small doses of tincture internally help in menstrual difficulties, menopausal liver sluggishness or stuckness, and winter depression

(SAD). Calendula is also widely available in a great variety of homeopathic formulations. Fortunately, calendula is easy to grow in many regions and makes a cheering indoor winter plant partner in cold weather climates.

*True calendula is sometimes called pot marigold, but is not to be confused or replaced with the garden ornamental marigolds (*Tagetes spp.*).

© *Billie Potts 1994*

ħħħ

♎ sábado
16

☽□♂	9:52 am
♃ApG	3:21 pm
♀☌♆	4:46 pm
♂□♇	4:48 pm

☉☉☉

♎ ♏ domingo
17

☽□♆	6:57 am	
☽□♀	8:20 am	
☉✳☽	8:54 am	
☽✳♃	10:35 am	
☽□♅	2:41 pm	v/c
☽→♏	5:08 pm	

After The Storm

There is a joy
beyond words
which comes when the hurricane dies –

a deep peace in the heart
and a quiet elation
that joins with everything around.

We have weathered the storm –
we have survived.

Damage there may be,
but in the stillness
one knows
that it could have been worse –

we *are* still here –
all that matters is still here –
and the joy in our hearts
is the knowing
of the things that do matter.
The dross falls away.

The winter sun smiles weakly
and lights the torn and sodden world
with gold.

We pause
and breathe freely again
with the birds and the animals
with the trees and the earth herself.
Relief of silence
after the battering.
Soon may come another onslaught,
but for the moment
in the heart of the moment
there is peace and strength
and the joy of knowing
that which is truly real.

La Madre

© *Marsha A. Gomez 1991*

December

♏ Monday
18

D✶♉ 10:48 am
☉♂♃ 1:44 pm
D✶♂ 5:08 pm

♏ Tuesday
♐ 19

D△♄ 12:42 am
D✶♆ 9:52 am
D✶♀ 3:40 pm
D✶♅ 5:08 pm v/c
D→♐ 7:14 pm
D♂♇ 9:43 pm

♐ Wednesday
20

♀□♇ 1:43 am
♀♂♅ 9:50 am

♐ Thursday
♑ 21

D□♄ 1:09 am
♀→♒ 10:24 am
D♂♃ 2:23 pm v/c
☉♂D 6:23 pm
D→♑ 6:47 pm

New Moon in ♐ Sagittarius 6:23 pm PST
2:23 GMT

♑ Friday
22

Solstice

☉→♑ 12:18 am
DPrG 2:04 am
♀✶♇ 6:16 pm
D♂♉ 9:33 pm
D♂♂ 9:57 pm

Sun in Capricorn 12:18 am PST, 8:18 GMT

All aspects in Pacific Standard Time; add 3 hours for EST; add 8 hours for GMT

□ Monica Sjöö 1987

Winter Solstice

The light returns as the sun shifts and starts to move northward again. We look within ourselves now to find the new source of light and regeneration.

At the time of the Winter Solstice, the sun appears to stand still for four days. Native Americans refer to this time period as Earth Renewal and spend the four days in prayer and fasting, remaining close to nature and refraining from many activities, in order to give the earth a rest and pray for the sun to move on.

In Europe, the tradition of the yule log is celebrated on Winter Solstice. A special log is brought in and placed on the hearth where it glows for the twelve nights of the holiday season. After that, it is kept in the house all year to protect the home and its inhabitants from illness and any adverse conditions. The yule log is the counterpart of the midsummer bonfires, which were held outdoors on Summer Solstice. It is also customary to place mistletoe around the fire, which is the plant that grew on the oak tree, sacred to the Druids, the priests of the Celts. Mistletoe has many uses and is thought to help women to conceive. The Christmas tree also dates from old European or pagan rituals; it was the time to celebrate the renewal of all earth, and greens were used as the symbol – branches of pine, cedar, and juniper. Red candles are symbolic of the fire returning, the fire and heat of the sun as the days begin to lengthen.

© Marcia Starck 1993, printed and excerpted from <u>Women's Medicine Ways:</u>
<u>Cross-Cultural Rites of Passage</u> with permission from The Crossing Press.

We'Moon Move Forward in Tyme   ◻ *Oriol Dancer 1994*

**Meditation for
Mother Earth**

*Pick a toxic waste site.
Imagine hundreds of women gathered together
Ritually pouring buckets of menstrual blood
Directly onto this wounded part of our sacred planet.*

*Picture
The mega-nutrients from women's blood
Seeping their way into the pores,
The veins, the bowels,
Into the very consciousness
Of Mother Earth Herself.*

Visualize deep, primordial healing.

Selene Circle (named for one of the Greek moon goddesses) was a menstrual circle I belonged to. We met on the new moon of each month. One month we were unable to convene, so instead we did a "psychic circle." For ten minutes at an agreed upon day and hour, we channeled our collective gynergy into the universe and envisioned this poem.   ◻ *Cathleen McGuire, Selene Circle*

Dream of Freedom

I DREAM OF FREEDOM
I dream of being free from racist remarks, stares, harassment and the possibility of being harmed
because of my skin color
free of people who
make excuses for racism
free to any
sexual preference I choose
free to walk at night
and not be scared
free to do with my body
as I see fit
free of stereotypes
free of classism, sexism
and racism
free of laws and rules
that dictate and separate
free to see and accept
people for who they are,
and not judge them by
the color of their skin
free to be me and
not what society dictates
free to have a dream
THE DREAM OF
FREEDOM
◻ *Laura Irene Wayne 1991*

◻ *Monica Sjöö 1972*

***Women Have Only Their
Chains to Lose***

ʰʰʰ

♑
♒
Saturday
23

☽⚹♄	12:19 am
☿☌♂	5:42 am
☽☌♆	8:59 am
☽☌♅	4:09 pm v/c
☽→♒	5:53 pm
☽⚹♇	8:33 pm
☽☌♀	10:50 pm

☉☉☉

♒ ◑
Sunday
24

☿⚹♄	2:56 am
♂⚹♄	11:50 pm

Dezember

♒︎
♓︎

Montag
25

☽﹡♃　3:36 pm　v/c
☽→♓︎　6:46 pm
☽□♇　9:43 pm

♓︎

Dienstag
26

☉﹡☽　1:45 am

♓︎
♈︎

Mittwoch
27

☽♂♄　3:39 am
☽﹡♂　6:33 am
☽﹡♅　11:55 am
☽﹡♆　1:16 pm
☽□♃　8:36 pm
☽﹡♅　9:33 pm　v/c
☽→♈︎　11:07 pm

♈︎

Donnerstag
28

♅♂♆　1:29 am
☽△♇　2:26 am
☉□☽　11:08 am
☽﹡♀　3:25 pm

Waxing Half Moon in ♈︎ Aries 11:08 am PST, 19:08 GMT

♈︎

Freitag
29

☽□♂　5:16 pm
☽□♆　9:00 pm

All aspects in Pacific Standard Time; add 3 hours for EST; add 8 hours for GMT

Moonsister with Snowball

Self Love

I met a cat by my back door. She'd watch me. She took a long time to risk coming near. Then if I moved, she'd dart away. Sometimes, though, she'd let me curl my fingers through her grey fur. More rarely still, and warily, she'd purr.

She seemed to prefer the dark... but at times enjoyed to roll and stretch in the sun and glance at me.

I wouldn't see her for days, or weeks. Or months. But she always came back.

Self love crept up on me like this shy cat.

© *Roseanna Waters 1992*

ħħħ

♈
♉ 🌓 Samstag
30

☽□♅	1:59 am	
☽△♃	5:44 am	
☽□♅	5:57 am	v/c
☽→♉	7:22 am	

☉☉☉

♉ 🌓 Sonntag
31

☉△☽	1:18 am
☽□♀	7:05 am
☿♂♅	8:34 pm
☽⚹ħ	9:24 pm

janvier 1996

☽☽☽

♉ ♊ lundi 1

☽△♂ 7:53 am
☽△♆ 7:55 am
♂☌♆ 8:27 am
☿→♒ 10:07 am
♀△⚷ 11:33 am
☽△♅ 5:19 pm v/c ☽△☿ 7:21 pm
☽→♊ 6:30 pm ☽☍♇ 10:29 pm

♂♂♂

♊ mardi 2

♃→♑ 11:23 pm

☿☿☿

♊ mercredi 3

☽△♀ 1:49 am
☽□♄ 9:54 am v/c
☿⚹♇ 9:59 am

♃♃♃

♊ ♋ jeudi 4

☽→♋ 6:57 am
☽☍♃ 7:33 am
☉□⚷ 12:41 pm

♀♀♀

♋ vendredi 5

☽ApG 3:33 am
☉☍☽ 12:52 pm
☽△♄ 10:54 pm

Full Moon in ♋ Cancer 12:52 pm PST, 20:52 GMT

All aspects in Pacific Standard Time; add 3 hours for EST; add 8 hours for GMT

Winter Healing

I finally Love Myself
Enough
that I am choosing to face
and heal
this excruciating pain.
It is not courage,
not bravery,
nothing but Love
that allows me to finally face my pain.
And this pain is so profound
and so deep
and has roots so deep
that they go down into my Soul
my cells,
my Spirit being.
But now it is Time to Start
    uprooting the Pain.
Time to make room for something else
in the now fertile, deep, rich soil.
Time to pull the tree out by its roots,
time to mourn its loss
and all the pain it represents.

Time to stare down into the empty
    holes
where the roots once were
and see deep, barren earth
with rocks and sticks
    and earthworms poking through.
See raw pain,
bones of the Earth,
Myself.
Time to feel the gaping wounds
in the Motherground of myself.
Cry a river of tears.
And heal.
Heal myself.
And it is a time to pour crystals
and plant seeds
in this fragile, healing soil of myself.
To gently pat the earth over
the delicate tiny seeds.
Pray for their growth.
Bless & nourish them with my tears.
Wait,
and let Nature take her course.

□ Jennifer Rose Crowwomyn 1992

_____ ካካካ _____

♋
♌   ◐   samedi
              6

☽♂♆   9:14 am
☽♂♂   5:19 pm
☽♂♅   6:55 pm   v/c
☽→♌   7:31 pm
☽△♇   11:51 pm

_____ ⊙⊙⊙ _____

♌   ◐   dimanche
              7

☽♂♉   4:54 am
♂♂♅   7:39 pm

The Blessing

© Nancy Bright 1987

COVER NOTES

Front Cover by Julie Higgins, "Healing Hands / Healing Heart" © 1992:

In my most recent series of work I am dealing with "Heart Healing" – a symbolic journey on healing the Heart – how the Heart transforms pain, how we transform and grow in our relationships with others and with the Planet. The various symbols of Ravens and Fish and Snakes within a landscape, along with the suggestion of figure in the central part, illustrate the cycles and rhythms of all life forms. The transformation of the Heart, how it connects with and relates to everything we encounter in life, is what inspires this series.

© Julie Higgins 1994

Back Cover by Nancy Bright, "The Healing" © 1986:

Nancy Bright is a self-taught watercolor artist who began self-publishing her work in 1987, creating a home-based mail-order business through which her greeting cards and prints are now distributed nationally and abroad. Nancy's work includes a variety of themes and styles, but the work that is closest to her heart (which she considers her "real" art) are images from the *Journey's* series. These images are inspired by thoughts and emotions born out of personal life experience, dreams, and visions – reflections of her inner spirit. For a brochure on Nancy's work, please send SASE to PO Box 11451, Eugene, OR 97470.

© Nancy Bright 1994

ACKNOWLEDGMENTS

I would like to give special acknowledgment to Beth and Pandora, who coordinated the creation of **We'Moon '95** (Beth on graphics; Pandora on writings). They did a wonderful job of pulling together **We'Moon** weaving circles, the Moon themes, art, and writing in the true spirit of **We'Moon**. Extra bouquets go to Beth, who after three years of **We'Moon** work has grown into the job of "We'Moonager"! She takes care of the ongoing business of Mother Tongue Ink and is the one most likely to answer your calls and letters. It is a great joy to discover that I am not indispensable after all (almost) and that there is a new generation of we'moon coming along to help carry on the work of **We'Moon** in such a good way. I also want to thank the feature writers (Gretchen Lawlor, Billie Potts) and other we'moon who contribute such beautiful works of art year after year (that this little book cannot possibly do justice to). My thanks also to Francis for taking us through the desktop publishing hurdles – including two marathons this year. As always, I am grateful for the community of womyn on and around womyn's land in Oregon, who form the living Goddess matrix out of which **We'Moon** grows.

Musawa 1994

I'd like to acknowledge Musawa for entrusting me with the care of the **We'Moon** for this year. I feel honored. Thanks Mu, for the guidance and insight you share.

Plentitudes of gratitude go out to the amazing womyn who wove the WM: Catherine, Diana, Ila, Judith, Mira, Laurel, Patience, Kaseja, Caroline, Madrone, Bethroot, Deah, Kirsten, Amy, Dana, Carrie, and Carruch.

Special thanks to Bethroot and Madrone for hosting our southern Oregon weaving circle and Judith for hosting our Portland circle. Deep appreciation goes to those who astutely proofread the WM: Pandora, Carruch, Lori, Mira, Maureen, Ila, gani et se, Julie, Annie O., Little Sun, and Justine.

Thanks to Gisela Ottmer and Rosemarie Merkel for once again translating and so generously producing the German edition.

Much appreciation is felt for all the networking/logistical support: Jemma Crae (for the last cycle of the recycled loan), Nancy and Jeri of In Her Image Gallery in Portland, Oregon (for helping us network with artists), the womyn at Rainbow's End (for graciously hosting the pagemaking stage of production at their beautiful home), Gitta and Cherie (for their nourishing support during **WM** and yurt production), Margarita Donnelly of Calyx Books (for sharing publishing wisdom and experience), and Laverne Lewis (for her accounting magic and counsel). © *Beth Freewomon 1994*

CREDIT / COPYRIGHTS / CONTACT

Please honor the copyrights of the following **We'Moon** contributors. © means *do not reproduce without the expressed permission of the artist or author.* Some we'moon prefer to free the copyright on their work. ¤ means *this work may be passed on among we'moon who wish to reprint it "in the spirit of the Mother Tongue" (with credit given and a copy sent to the author/artist when possible).* Contributors can be contacted directly when their addresses are given in the bylines, or by writing to Mother Tongue Ink, P.O. Box 1395 Estacada, OR 97023, USA with a stamped envelope plus $1.00 each for handling. **We'Moon** networking is welcomed!

CONTRIBUTOR BYLINES

Alise Ariel (Lambertville, NJ) has written screenplays and stories, published poems, textbook writing, newspaper features, and astrology articles and amazingly did this while remaining virtually income-free! She is also an artist and Tarot reader.

Alma Luz Villanueva (Santa Cruz, CA): Author of *Bloodroot; Mother, May I?; Life Span; Planet* – poetry. *The Ultraviolet Sky* (republished with Doubleday, May 1993, won an American Book Award); *Naked Ladies* (Arizona State University, June 1993) – novels. Mother of 3 sons and 1 daughter, 2 grandchildren.

Ann Hemdahl-Owen (Waddy, KY): Painter, art therapist, professor. I paint to know myself and my world.

Ann Snyder Bajovich (Gleneden Beach, OR) is an artist and college instructor. I use elements dealing with personal and social issues. I use imagery that addresses life and the human condition.

Annie Ocean (Lesbian Land, Rosebud, OR) is a radical country lesbian, naturalist, goddess worshiper, sufi, photographer, herbalist, tradeswoman and quintuplet water sign witch.

Becca Butcher Schoenfliess (Baltimore, MD): Artist, writer, lowland prowler by winter, mountain dweller in summer, playing on a book, An Artist at Living.

Berta Freistadt (London, UK) lives in a belfry overlooking a cemetery. The trees and ghosts are good neighbors but there's not much to be said for the squirrels. Being cute just isn't enough. But poetry is being written and health improves – so what's to grumble about.

Beth Freewomon (We'Moon Healing Ground, Estacada OR): I'm just at the foothills of my Saturn return (10th house). I'm clarifying how I'm out in the world. Also deepening into my inner landscape, doing *the* work. After three years in one place, my roots are sinking further into this beautiful and endangered Earth. Still an over-extended multi-talented witchy dyke!

Bev Severn (Denman Island, BC, Canada): I live on a beautiful island in British Columbia with my daughter, Alana. My sculptural and decorative claywork reflects my love of nature and celebrates the creativity of the Goddess within.

Billie Potts (Summit, NY) is an herbalist, lesbian feminist health activist, and author of *Witches Heal: Lesbian Herbal Self-Sufficiency; Ergonomics: A Problem Solver's Handbook; A New Woman's Tarot;* and the forthcoming *Herbal Diversity: the Earth Road.*

Boa Snake ♀: (Owl Farm, OR) As potter, painter, poet, I draw from deep within me images which speak to and of me. My art is a celebration of our womyn's power.

Boudykke (Minneapolis, MN) is an irreverent fat dyke of Italian, French, and English descent. Her hobbies are trying to outsmart the patriarchy and looking toward a lesbian future.

Carole Shaw (Brighton, England): I am an art therapist and teacher working with women who have been sexually abused in childhood. My art work explores my own experiences.

Caroline Brumleve (Boulder Creek, CA): Dreamer, word-weaver, changling/ seedling from ancient memory, embracing the grit and grace of the universe through dance, writing, ritual, and loving, all-eyes-open existence.

Carolyn McTaggart (Nelson, BC, Canada): I can turn my hand to most anything. A lot of 3-D these days, expressing herstory and delving into mythologies and our memories. I may actually stay in one place for awhile now, here in the Kootenays, surrounded by mountains.

Catherine Firpo (San Francisco, CA): Native of the Bay Area, she has been leading workshops and classes in both Creativity and Meditation for four years. Catherine has a B.A. in Art, and exhibits locally. Certified in therapeutic massage, and has trained in healing, intuition, and shamanism.

Cathleen McGuire (Minneapolis, MN) has found a path of healing through radical ecofeminist activism. She recently moved from New York City to Minneapolis where she works with the artist Jane Evershed.

Christine Pierce (Corvallis, OR): I am an earth-loving lesbian growing into my power, my love, my rage, my creative visions, and my miraculous healing potentialities.

Debby Earthdaughter (Saguaroland, Tucson, AZ): 32, European heritage, from middle class, living on SSI with multiple chemical sensitivity. Emerging from satanic ritual abuse.

Deborah Koff Chapin (Langley, WA): Has been developing and teaching the process of touch drawing since it was revealed to her in ecstatic play in 1974. Co-author, with Marcia Lauck, of *At the Pool of Wonder* (Bear & Co.). Her work is available at In Her Image Gallery in Portland, Oregon.

Deborah Winter (Molalla, OR): I am an artist and teacher on a healing journey with the help of the forest where I live, the animals and spirits and healing waters that I share this sacred space with.

Demetra George (Waldport, OR): Feminist astrologer and mythologist, is the author of *Asteroid Goddesses, Astrology for Yourself,* and *Mysteries of the Dark Moon.* She has lectured nationally and internationally, and currently is the director of the Oregon Coast Center for Women's Studies.

Denise Ann Fortier (Eugene, OR): I am a womyn/artist/teacher/student. I live with my partner and my cat and a baby-to-be in a house in the country. I am lucky to be surrounded by the beauty of nature.

Diana A. Cohen (Portland, OR) is a lesbian poet and carpenter. She's had work published in numerous journals including *The Spoon River Poetry Review* and in two anthologies.

Diana Rose Hartwoman (Northridge, CA) writes, paints and works for the EIA (Evolutionary Intelligence Agency), a Gaia-loving club open to any responsive individual who passes an easy entrance exam. She is currently working on a collection of essays for invoking post-modern faces of the Goddess and believes that it's women's work to guide civilization back to bliss.

Draak (Portland, OR): I am a fierce woman, nature Lover, a witch, and Artist. We are comprised of 18+ personalities – (alters) – selves. We are currently surviving patriarchal art school. Blessed Be!

Durga Bernhard (Woodstock, NY) is a painter, printmaker, graphic designer and illustrator of numerous children's books. Her work has been influenced by ancient and tribal art from all over the world.

Erica Owens (Gainesville, FL): I am an eccentric Libran animal lover and witch, American of Irish roots, who prizes good conversation over a hot cup of coffee. I am trying to teach myself Irish Gaelic, and I welcome both advice and "pen pals" in that or any other language.

Frances Bean Sidhe (Vancouver, BC, Canada): I am a poet, rune reader and lesbian. My poems are memory, healing and hope for the future.

Frances Finley (Edmonton, Canada): I am a northern womyn who expresses the Goddess and her rhythms in my art, sculpture, writing, and rituals. I'm also a proud survivor of incest and other patriarchal scars, in recovery for four years.

Francesca Thoman (Mountain View, CA): I'm 40 years alive, round at the edges, happily married and susceptible to joy and magic. My poems ask to be written when they want to be spoken. Otherwise it's sci-fi and children's stories.

Genece Klein (Vancouver, WA) is an illustrator and graphic designer who has shown her work at regional galleries.

Gentle Doe (Truth or Consequences, NM): Poet, ceremonialist, artist, dancer, spiritual therapist, honoring and celebrating light, all life. I ride waves of laughter, softening, sweeping the heart's chambers.

Grace Silvia (Carlton, OR): Euro-Jewish Lesbian. Having a wonderful Saturn return. Always talked to plants and animals. Now learning to listen to them. Blessed be.

Gretchen Lawlor (Langley, WA): An astrologer and naturopath, with a focus upon homeopathy and Flower Essences. I write, teach, and consult deep oracles through tea leaves. I have returned to my astrological practice and do horoscopes, taped readings and phone consultations. If you are interested, contact me at PO Box 753, Langley, WA 98260.

Gwyneth (B. C. Rowley) (Victoria, BC, Canada): I am a Moon-in-Pisces Crone, mother, grandmother, professional poet/writer, and amateur artist.

Ila Suzanne (Portland, OR): Pisces, working class, white, lesbian, witch, poet, now turning toward crone. My work appears in lesbian publications. I am presently collaborating with Kay Gardner on *Ouroboros*, a choral and orchestral work on the stages in women's lives.

Jane Orleman (Ellensburg, WA): My current autobiographical work addresses the effects of physical and sexual violence towards children. In 1990, I found that the only escape from my creative block was to paint the truth of my life experiences. Many of the images are painted in a childlike rendition of actual memories. Others painted with palette or butcher knives express emotions long suppressed.

Jennifer Rose Crowwomyn (Olympia, WA): I am an Herbalist and proud Witch discovering the artist within and without. My work is a reflection of my Healing – a deep, transformational and sometimes painful process. I seek to Honor, recognize, embody, and Create Beauty in this life. Be In Beauty!

Jennifer Lynn Shafer (Olympia, WA): I am a white, anti-racist bisexual Taurean born on the full moon. I am healing from sexual abuse and separation from our Mother. I do this through love, rage and honesty, my radio show, crisis work with womyn and unlearning hate and relearning truth.

Jill Smith (Isle of Lewis, UK): Artist and poet of the spirit of ancient stones and landscape, journeying the paths between them; live with my young son and exhibit my work here. Visitors welcome! Tigh-a-ghlinne, Gravir, Isle of Lewis, Western Isles of Scotland, UK.

Jing (Olympia, WA): I am a multi-media artist, gemini, dreamer, and lover of the moon. I am on the path of self-discovery and would like to share my adventures and inspirations.

Jody Turner (Portland, OR): Creating artwork is my connection to my <u>self</u>. It is speaking my language to the world. As a child this comforted and empowered me. The images I create come from deep within and remind me of what I truly am.

Joules (Lopez Island, WA) is a woods-dwelling, beach-combing, fire-drumming songstress, devoted to the sister circle and to the healing of this sacred Earth and all of her creatures. Tapes of my songs are available from me (PO Box 153, Lopez Is., WA 98261).

Judith Anderson (East Lansing, MI): I make the images I need to see. Reinterpreting various myths, legends, and religious traditions in my etchings, I want to express women's power and feelings and the sacred nature of ordinary experience. *Medusa Unwound* represents my rage at the vilification and brutal treatment of woman.

Judith Burros (Portland, OR): Artist, quilter, photographer, survivor, searcher, finder of memories . . .

Julia Doughty (San Diego, CA): Writes poetry and performance art, and explores the wild spaces of the West Coast.

Julie Higgins (Mendocino, CA): I see the landscape, earth, and the body as vessels of life. Images of Ravens as goddess protectors express my concern for and connection with the planet.

Kathryn A. Rosenfeld (Yellow Springs, OH): I am a 1993 graduate of Antioch College with a degree in art. I'm a printmaker and photographer, and a lesbian-feminist witch.

Kirsty O'Connor (West Yorks, England): Living in the Yorkshire Pennines and juggling with creating, parenting, and paying the bills! Postcards available from "Moving Lines," Northlight Studios, Melbourne Works, Hebden Bridge, HX7 6AS, England.

Kiwani (Waletown, BC, Canada): Single mother of daughters living on rented land quietly learning patience; drumming for dyke land base in Western Canada, welcome correspondence and visitǫrs.

Lark Hajdu (Stamford, CT): I am a student of the Craft guided by instinct.

Laura Irene Wayne (San Diego, CA): Is a painter, printmaker, graphic artist, poet, writer, and illustrator of children's books. Laura's artwork reflects the heritage, culture, and experiences of her people and their environment.

Leslie Foxfire Stager (Portland, OR) is a rites of passage guide, seeking wisdom through birthing, deathing, touching, Hunting Spirit, stalking fear, and dancing in the moonlight.

Lillian Pitt (Portland, OR): Tsagaglalal overlooked the village where my great-grandparents lived. The village is beneath the Dalles dam floodwaters since 1957, wiping out a 10,000 year history.

Lois S. Bresee (So. Burlington, VT): I am poet, journal-keeper, artist in fabric wall hangings; I am a sojourner through life, one who wanders the edges and the in-between spaces, a gatherer of loose and raveled threads. . . always in search of WomanSpirit, of Feminine Wisdom.

Lorraine Lucie Lagimodière (Denman Island, BC, Canada): Person practicing the manifestation of inner vision through walking, talking, thinking, feeling, drawing, writing, meeting, and transforming materials already extracted from mother earth: May we rest in her peace.

Marcia Cohee (Laguna Beach, CA): I live in Laguna Canyon with husband Pat and daughter Devin. We host the Laguna Poets weekly reading series. My two books, *Sexual Terrain* and *Laguna Canyon Was Once a River*, are available from me at PO Box 249, Laguna Beach, CA 92652.

Marcia Starck (Santa Fe, NM): Author of *Women's Medicine Ways, The Dark Goddess – Dancing with the Shadow* and other books, is a medicine teacher blending the earth wisdom of the Goddess with rituals from Native American traditions and other cultures. She is also a Medical Astrologer and healer who incorporates nutrition, herbs, crystals, and other modalities in her work.

Marcy Marchello (Wendell, MA) is an artist, naturalist, and educator. She creates cards and stationery on recycled paper. For a free catalog, write to her c/o Earth Graphics, Box 262, Wendell, MA 01379.

Margaret De Maria (Occidental, CA): I see the enchantment beyond the obvious and seek to reveal the mysteries of nature where amazing things whisper into a willing ear and open the hearts and minds of all I share it with.

Mari Jackson (Nacogdoches, TX): I'm a witch whose craft is her art.

Mari Susan Selby (Santa Fe, NM): My work comes out of my great love of the earth and women. I'm in the process of writing a book on survival of sexual abuse. I'm really excited. I'm an astrologer and therapist by trade.

Marianna Crawford (Portland, OR): I work with clay and talk to my friends on the phone.

Marie Theodore (London, England): I am an actress, singer, and dancer. I have a desire to explore sacred drama in the context of healing our fragmented selves. I am currently taking a course to train as a priestess and devotee of Isis – the Great Goddess.

Marie Truscott (Cedar Falls, IA): A long time moonlodge sister. Grew up in the southwest desert; lived in the emerald northwest; and is now living in the heartland. Currently writing and creating with clay, beads, watercolors, and other mediums. Lives with Hank, her beautiful husband and their cat, Lucy, who is quite grand! Please do stop by: 2009 Oakland, Cedar Falls, IA 50613.

Marj Johnston (Cooloorta, Ireland): I'm 40, living on top of two fairy forts and experiencing a life of death and rebirth. I'm a tarot reader, gardener, and herbalist living in constant contact with fairies and earth spirits.

Marja de Vries (Amsterdam, Netherlands): I try to develop my writing skill, make patchwork, and enjoy working in my garden.

Marna Hauk (Pacific Cascadia Bioregion): A wild ♀ revolutionary poet artist coming into her power, taking time to heal herself as part of the planet. Blessed be the land. Always looking for womynly connection, pen pals, etc. Contact me at PO Box 14194, Portland, OR 97214.

Marsha A. Gomez (Austin, TX): Clay sculptor, environmental/human rights activist for 20 years. Currently director of Alma de Mujer Retreat Center for Social Change.

Mary Mackey (Berkeley, CA) has recently spent time in Brazil studying women's rituals. She is a novelist as well as a poet and has a particularly strong interest in environmental issues.

Mau Blossom (Doniphan, MO): I'm an emerging spirit who is an ecologist by nature and a health care provider who embraces Ayurvedic principles in her life as well as her practice. I am a musician – currently learning to play sax, piano, silver flute, and clarinet. I believe we need to heal the world by healing ourselves as completely as possible.

Megaera (Victoria, Australia) is a white lesbian-feminist artist living in Australia, who is committed to developing images which empower women and represent us lovingly.

Megan Vafis (Chico, CA): I am a 30 year old Lesbian who works in the Oregon woods part of the year, making my art the rest of the year. I am a survivor of family rape and battery; Lesbian sexual, physical, and emotional abuse and acquaintance sexual assault. I am in the process of remembering and healing. Making art helps me to do both.

Megan Wilson (Somerville, MA): I am a social deviant: feminist, anarchist, bisexual, witch, environmentalist, animal and human rights activist. The images in my work are a reflection of my social deviance.

Melissa Harris (Olivebridge, NY): Painter, Teacher, Healer, Astrologer continually trying to find innovative ways of combining all of the above. Grateful for life, my lover, her music, four cats and a dog.

Monica Sjöö (Bristol, UK): I am an artist and an author. I recently wrote *New Age and Armageddon: the Goddess or the Gurus?* Doing slide shows and workshops about my artwork. I also write for the *From the Flames* journal.

Musawa (We'Moon Healing Ground, OR): Opening my life for the Goddess to come through... takes a little more time than I thought. Hopefully, I will have gotten off on my "year off" by the time you read this, and be on my way from now "on."

Nance Paternoster (San Francisco, CA): I am a fine artist – a computer art technician. I've been working with computer graphics for 13 years. I am searching to create work which is a "healing experience" to the viewer.

Nancy Ann Jones (La Crescenta, CA): I am a teacher of Dianic Wicca, artist, writer/poet, shaky warrior, High Priestess of Our Lady of the West, mother and grandmother, coven sister, and much more.

Nancy Bright (Springfield, OR): Self-taught watercolor artist creating from emotion • heart • experience • I publish greeting cards and prints of my work. PO Box 11451, Eugene, OR 97440.

Nicola Beechsquirrel (S. Wales, UK): I am an artist celebrating through my paintings the sacredness of women's lives and cycles. Through my art, I empower myself and, I hope, other women.

Nikki Cash (Santa Cruz, CA): I'm a humyn animal spirited lesbian artist. I live in a mecca of lesbians and artists. My work is inspired by love and the great goddess mother earth.

Oriol Dancer (Medstead, SASK, Canada): These days find me grieving for the loss of what has been – the nights, dreaming futures of harmonious right relationship with all creation. Art is the balancing one heart medicine.

Pamela EH! (Portland, OR): I am a mother, a poet, and a collective member of Laughing Horse Books. I am comforted by the endurance and change of Mother Earth. My most powerful totems are Turtle and Bear. They have helped heal me from chronic depression and substance abuse.

Pamela A. Grout (Chicago, IL): I'm a creative and spiritual person that is deeply moved by women's rituals. I'm a fiber artist trying to find my voice through my art and contact with other women. I'm a menopausal woman finding I love myself, husband, family and friends more each day. Blessed be!

Pandora (We'Moon Healing Ground, OR): i am a grass roots amazon earth fairy, full of leo fire, and mountains. i try constantly to help heal this earth with words, love, laughter and laying of hands. in sisterhood . . . in peace and revolution.

Peni Hall (Berkeley, CA) is a disabled artist and videographer. Her artwork often reflects the many facets of living with disability and chronic illness.

Pesha Gertler (Seattle, WA): Lives in Seattle surrounded by mountain muses, the Olympics and Cascades. In this environment, she teaches and writes poetry and prose.

Rachel Bachman (Seattle, WA): I am an animator, artist, musician, and poet. I enjoy combining my talents. I have made two animated film poems.

Rashani (Na'Alehu Ka'u, HI) has recently recorded her 14th audio cassette and currently has over 180 card designs distributed in several countries. She is co-founder of Earthsong community in Hawaii and teaches workshops and gives concerts throughout the world.

Red Raven (Torrance, CA): Spiral journaler, mural painter, channeler of poetry, creatrix of Goddess images for Her altar, Heaver of Mountains – Digger of Spirit in the Circle of the Wild Yoni Hairs.

Roia Ferragallo (Berkeley, CA): An aspiring video and film producer, Roia is 25 and works at a broadcast station in Oakland, California. She seeks to express her own healing from childhood sexual abuse through watercolor painting, poetry, and counseling. She had her first child in 1993.

Roseanna Waters (London, England): I am a survivor of childhood rape and torture by most of my family, which I began remembering and working on in 1986. Six years on I wonder when healing will be less of a struggle, it seems to continue to expand and go deeper, touching wounds that go way beyond myself. However this helps me keep going, knowing how much the earth needs us to learn love, truth, and connection.

Roxanne Firewind (Brattleboro, VT): I am 38. I was a truck mechanic with my boyfriend who was violent and sexually abusive in South Dakota. We built a beautiful addition and planted and cared for 45 trees. Now I live in Vermont with a 24 year old composer and song writer. I believe the goddess is the second coming. I am an astrologer, writer, singer, and cellist.

S.J. Hugdahl (Forks of Salmon, CA): I'm living in Northern California with my family, my horse, the foxes, the salmon, the bear, the cougar, the jays, the eagles, the toads, my cat, the ringtails, the deer, the blackberries and my art.

Sandra Pastorius AKA Laughing Giraffe (Santa Cruz, CA): With awe and inspiration, I continue my practice of astrological counselling, and more recently metaphysical book selling at Gateway's Bookstore. For more information write: PO Box 2344, Santa Cruz, CA 95063.

Sheila Broun (West Yorkshire, England): Working with the goddess, sacred trees, and elemental forces.

Sherri Rose-Walker (Pacifica, CA): I am a collage artist and poet living on the foggy coast of California. My art is imaginal archaeology – excavating forgotten treasures of women's lives and spirituality. My poetry is my journal of transformations.

Shoshana Rothaizer (Flushing, NY): A native New Yorker who connects Mother Nature's rhythms and spirits both in city and country. She hopes that her photography serves as a bridge between people of different lifestyles. Brochure of her postcards available: 147-44 69th Rd., Flushing, NY 11367.

Sierra Lonepine Briano (Portland, OR): I am a 47 year old Lesbian artist, loud mouth and trouble maker. I recently survived the L.A. earthquake, so there shouldn't be much left to scare me. My astrologer says I'm a late bloomer and I like that because it means I can choose from my whole life experience when I paint. I am happily settled in Oregon where I am working on a new series of Goddesses I Have Known.

Sonja Shahan (Santa Cruz, CA): I live in the woods, where my soul sings strongest. My life is thick with religion, with spirals and seasons, with tree sap and rosemilk, with dreams and dance, fruit and fire. i grow, i heal, i create, and i dig my roots ever deeper.

Sudie Rakusin (Hillsborough, NC): Is an Aries with 5 other planets in Fire, an artist living with 2 dog companions in the woods surrounded by ever expanding gardens, dealing on a personal daily level with the major transformation going on in the universe.

Sue Lorentz (Columbia, MD) is a community activist, a teacher of meditation and alternative healing techniques, and a founder and director of Women's Healing and Empowerment, a non-profit organization whose goal is to empower women to make the changes necessary for personal development.

Susan Levitt (Sausalito, CA) is a teacher, wise woman, and priestess of Women's Mysteries. Her coven name is Mermaid. She reads Tarot Cards and can be reached at 415-331-1028 or 72B Girard Ave., Sausalito, CA 94965.

Suzanne Benton (Ridgefield, CT) is a day 1 feminist from the late '60s. A sculptor, mask performer (mask tales of women of myth, heritage) and printmaker, she has just returned from 10 1/2 months traveling (India, Europe, Ireland, Kenya, and Tanzania), sharing and creating from a feminist perspective.

Suzanne Ghiglia (Boulder, CO) leads writing groups and teaches flute lessons. She has devoted her life to encouraging people to empower themselves through creativity.

Sylph (Oakland, CA): Lesbian separatist born in England, cross class (poverty class mother, middle class father), Jewish, and Celtic ancestry. Asthmatic since girlhood.

Tamara Thiebaux (Wolfville, Nova Scotia): My work radiates from personal healing, and concern for social, ecological and spiritual issues. I delight in inspiring fresh perspective and challenging negative social attitudes.

Tee A. Corinne (Sunny Valley, OR): Artwork and writing have been published in the Women's Movement Press since 1974.

Terri L. Jewell (Lansing, MI): Black Lesbian Feminist winner of 1994 creative artist grant for poetry from Arts Foundation of Michigan and editor of *The Black Woman's Gumbo Ya-Ya: Quotations by Black Women* (The Crossing Press, 1993).

Tinker (Leaburg, OR): A painter of concepts, tinker's art has evolved in her endeavor to reach viewers "through their hearts and minds." Best known for her Native American work, tinker's interests vary to include fantasy, surrealism, and portraits. Currently working on Native American "Medicine" paintings.

Treelight Green (Santa Fe, NM) is a healer educator and artist who, since 1973, specializes in mind body whole brain integration and meditation. Treelight Productions has 4 nationally distributed audio cassettes of guided meditations available called *Breathing Is The Key Vol. I & II* and *Light Journeys: Exploring* and *Aligning the Chakras.*

Vicki Blake (Bonners Ferry, ID) enjoys living on a small acreage with her husband Jack and two sons Zachary and Benjamin. She works as a choreographer and performer in musical theater and opera, as well as retailing birch bark creations, bead art, and photography in the form of greeting cards.

Vicki Ledray Grabicki (Issaquah, WA): I paint ancient memories, ones that we all share. As my process evolves, my recurring themes are birth, life, nature. As paintings, they work as gateways, giving spirit an anchor in the physical world. This allows the healing energy of the image to flow into our lives, effecting change and transformation.

Vicki Moser (Portland, OR) works as a graphic artist.

Z (suzsanna) Budapest (Oakland, CA) works on her books and *13th Heaven,* her TV show about the goddess.

zana (Tucson, AZ): 46, disabled jew living on land-trust land. a collection of my poetry and line drawings, *herb womon,* is available for $7 (more/less or barter) from me at 12101 w. calle madero, tucson, az 85743.

Zetta Bear (W. Yorkshire, England): I strive to live passionately, boldly, and with generosity of spirit, but quite often I stay in and watch T.V. instead.

"Spirit Bath" © *Tinker 1989*

Call for Contributions

We'Moon '96: Earth Matters

Earth Actions, Earth Art, Earth Changes, Endangered Earth, Healing Earth, Embodying Spirit, Relating to the Material Plane, Duality, Healing the Splits, Heaven and Earth, Deep Ecology, Indigenous Peoples, Gaia. **Materials Already Due: Sept. 21, 1994**

NOW ACCEPTING CONTRIBUTIONS FOR:

We'Moon '97: Womyn in Community

Womyn's community, womyn's lands, womyn's culture; womyn in relation to each other: lesbian, hetero, bi-sexual, sisters, sangha, friends, lovers, family, tribe; cross cultures, class, age, race, country, city. What kinds of communities are womyn creating? Are we getting what we want? Herstory, alternative models, stuck places, breakthroughs, strategies for survival, group structure and process, self and other, power and powerlessness, dealing with differences. What is working and what is not? Overturning the patriarchy... within and without... moving through obstacles, community building, politics, spirituality and healing, rituals of everyday life.

WE WELCOME YOUR ART AND BRIEF WRITINGS

Due Date: Sept. 21, 1995

Please note: **We'Moon** is an exploration of a world created in Her image. We welcome artwork by, for and about womyn. It is not by, for, or about men or womyn's relations to men. Our focus is on womyn only as an affirmation of the range and richness of a world where womyn are whole unto themselves. Many earth-based cultures traditionally have women-only times and places, which, through deepening the female experience, are seen to enhance women's contribution to the whole fabric of society. **We'Moon** invites all womyn who love and honor womyn to join us in this spirit, and we offer what we create from such a space for the benefit of all sentient beings.

To receive a Call for Contributions or further information, please send an SASE (a Self-Addressed Stamped Envelope or international postal coupon) to:

Mother Tongue Ink, P.O. Box 1395, Estacada, OR 97023

Matriarchal Astrology... and Other Variations

There is some evidence that there were 13 signs in some ancient **matriarchal zodiacs**, corresponding to the 13 Moons of the lunar calendar (the 13th sign is thought to be "Arachne," the spider, in between Taurus and Gemini). Hindu astrology uses 28-30 **lunar houses** as well as the 12 solar houses associated with the zodiac as we know it, and views each person's chart through both "eyes of heaven" (the Moon and the Sun) at once. Other eras undoubtedly used other **numerology** in dividing the pie of the sky: Virgo and Scorpio, for instance, were once merged together where Libra now is.

There are even two different versions of the zodiac based on the 12 star signs commonly used. The **Tropical Zodiac** uses the Earth-Sun cycle as its source, beginning with 0° Aries on the March Equinox; the **Sidereal Zodiac** uses the constellations' positions relative to earth as its source, which has drifted 29° backwards with the Precession of the Equinoxes (so the sun is said to be at 1° Pisces on the March Equinox). Like two clocks set to different time zones, both are valid. In this case, they seem to reflect different levels of reality. For example, when you plant by the ephemeris, using the Tropical Zodiac, you are encouraging growth in the vital physical-emotional energy fields; when you plant by the Sidereal Zodiac, you are speaking to the more subtle soul-spirit energies.

However you cut it, the sky encircles the earth, the planets move in cycles, and the signs describe a sequence of stages... in the movement of matter through space over time (e.g., energy). The 12 signs we use now are only one way of looking at it – we'moon are all the time redefining the signs and what they mean to us in the cycles of growth in our own lives.

In our currently **solar-dominated cultures**, when people ask: "What is your sign?" they generally mean your **Sun sign**. Remember that your **Moon sign** and **Rising sign** are just as important, and that every other planet has a sign in your natal chart as well. The qualities of the Zodiac Signs can be adapted to any planet, once you understand the kind of energy each planet channels in your life story. See "Sun Signs: Journey" pp. 18-20 and "Moon Signs: Transits" pp. 21-22.

Moon Nodes are another neglected part of we'moon astrology. They are the points of intersection where the orbits involving the Sun, Moon, and Earth meet. They are about relationships in our family of origin, our inner circle, the alignment of our self-will and cosmic-will, and are linked with eclipses on the new and full moons. In your chart, the North (☊) and South (☋) Nodes point out the direction of your karma, the "head and tail of the dragon," respectively. Their positions are given in the ephemeris charts in back.

Asteroids: See "Why Asteroids?" and "Asteroid Emphemeris" p. 202.

□ *Musawa*

LUNAR CHARTS: A NATIVE AMERICAN PERSPECTIVE

Native Astrology: Among other things, for many thousands of years, the art of reading the sky was lovingly taught by the elders to the younger generation. Because each old person knew different things, our elders were like a living library. We believe knowledge should not stagnate on a shelf, but be lovingly poured from one generation to another. Many libraries have burned, and books we never dreamed of were destroyed in ages past. But the things we needed to know survived by example. If all our astrology books were removed tomorrow, how many of you could go outside and find the zodiac around your house?

Know Your Moon: The real "heart" of this book is the Moon. It is the closest heavenly body and seems to exert a tremendous physical and emotional influence on us all.

Of the 13 lunations a year, there are three considered very important. The first is, of course, one's natal Moon position. Then it is extremely important to consider the last new Moon preceding the child's birth. The proximity of the prenatal lunation and house position show how clearly the person would know what their sense of direction is. It establishes the life goals, and is our ancestral roots.... The third most important Moon is the first full Moon after birth. The post-natal full Moon establishes further definitions of goals and how to accomplish them, and the circumstances at the end of life.

Lunar Charts: An interesting way to use the lunations and your Moon's position is to do a lunar chart every month. It is just like a solar chart, except you use the Moon and its degree to find the equal cusps. For example, if your Moon is 10° Libra, you put 10° Libra on the ascendant, then put 10° Scorpio on the 2nd House and 10° Sagittarius on the 3rd and so on. *Put your Moon on the ascendant.* Then go right across the ephemeris for the current date and take planets except for the Moon and insert them. Now add the new and full Moon. If something special is planned – do the chart for that day. This will give you a true emotional barometer – a monthly emotional, personal forecast.

Mexican Moon Goddess Tlazolteotl giving birth to herself as "The old moon gives birth to the new."

© *Marcy Marchello 1989*

© *Elisabeth Dietz Gauerke 1989, excerpted with permission from* The Medicine Road.

OUR COSMIC CLOCK
ASTROLOGICAL LIFE CYCLES

We all share common rites of passage at certain ages in our life cycle. Using the guidance of the Planet allies during these times can help us to understand the stresses, challenges, and unique opportunities that emerge as issues.

Our own planetary cosmic clock is set in motion at our birth when all the Planets begin their cycles. The time it takes for each Planet to then circle the Sun and return to its originating position determines one full cycle. These "return" times sound an "alarm" for us, and catalyze new phases of growth, change, and development throughout our ages and stages of life. Each Planet symbolizes certain life energies.

☉ When the SUN, symbol of the Self, returns to its original position each year we celebrate our "birthday." We may enjoy some extra attention, and a personal sense of renewal each year.

♂ The MARS cycle activates our ambitions every 2 years when it returns to the birth position. During these times we can re-energize our physical bodies, assert our passions, begin new projects, set business goals, and start therapies and programs for personal growth.

♃ JUPITER makes its first return at age 12 when we are at puberty and beginning a new phase of social growth. JUPITER then returns at ages 24, 36, 48, 60, 72 and 84. These ages offer us new confidence and opportunities for social and skill expansion. Career changes are best made at these times.

♄ SATURN takes 28-29 years for its first return to occur when our adulthood may be tested as we settle accounts, make commitments, and claim true inner authority. Saturn then returns at ages 56 and 84.

♅ URANUS has an orbit cycle of 84 years, completing one full revolution during what could be the complete human lifetime. Uranus catalyzes us to express our uniqueness, unfettered by conventions. It comes into trine (120°) aspect in its cycle each 28 years. We must respond to this call for creativity, while Saturn tempers these times with constraints, conditions, and responsibilities. With a restless, and often divine, discontent, we may break up old patterns and liberate ourselves from outworn situations. At approximately age 42, when Uranus comes into the 180° opposition phase, we may experience our own versions of the mid-life crisis.

Since we grow in spirals, these ages are often symbolically linked, and often we must deal with the new face of our life issues each time we experience a planetary return.

© *Sandra Pastorius 1993*

A RETURN TO SOURCE:
THE MERCURY ☿ ℞ RETROGRADE CYCLE

The cycle of the wing-footed messenger, Mercury, represents our mental and communicative life processes. This companion dancer to the Sun (never traveling more than 28° away) inspires mobility and adaptability within our environment. Through Mercury, we express ourselves with language, writing, speaking, and reasoning. At times, Mercury emerges in us as nimble jester or creative genius, or when in retrograde, the coyote trickster/teacher within. To this Muse of the Mind, we give thanks for our ability to grow in symbolic and intellectual connection with each other, and with ourselves.

Three or four times a year, always in one of the three signs ruled by the same element, Mercury goes retrograde. Due to the motion of the Earth's orbit, the planet *appears* to be moving backwards through zodiacal territory. During this passage lasting 20-28 days, our attentions move towards unfinished business. Since all backward movement symbolizes a return to source, we can use these times to attend to our inner perceptions, and reconnect with the spiritual source of our thoughts. This introversion can bring about a critical purification process that can help us gain new insights based on prior knowledge. These are good times for completing projects, connecting with old friends, and settling accounts. Delays often point towards the need for more attention to detail and rethinking priorities. Be patient and thorough. Take advantage of this ebb in the cycle. Daydream and rest more. When we linger longer to relish the ground beneath us, we can see the flowers blooming in the dust raised during our busy recent past.

In 1995, Mercury retrogrades three times, in each of the Air Signs. During Aquarius, from January 25-February 15 when Mercury reverses our synapses, we may use the sharp insight of Aquarius to explore ideas, and look for missing pieces in writing projects. While energies may feel scattered at times, refocus often. This is a good time to reconnect with old friends, and practice listening skills. During Gemini, from May 24-June 16 when Mercury retreats, find time to play with your inner child. Journaling or letter writing allows us to access memories and express undercurrents. During Libra, from September 22-October 13, when Mercury retraces her steps, the winds of change shift our perspectives, especially in relationships. Allow for inner dialogs to retrace intentions. Use process in your communications. Entertain old lovers.

Used consciously, we can turn this change in polarity of our mental life towards healing and renewal. When Mercury goes direct we can move ahead with new plans and projects, and put any mental values gleaned into play. Remember, Mercury is the channel through which we will send messages to our future Selves, and create the collaborative mental sharing to which we attribute our humanness.   © *Sandra Pastorius 1993*

Why Asteroids?

The discovery of the first asteroids points to the rebirth of the Goddess in women's spirituality. Traditional astrology uses only two planets to symbolize female archetypes: Moon as mother and Venus as mate. As a result, astrological language has tried to fit all other women's experiences into male-defined archetypes.

When a heavenly body is prominent in the sky at the time of a person's birth, the mythological story of the god or goddess who shares the same name as the planet or asteroid becomes a major theme in that individual's life.

Ceres, the Great Mother, provides a model to understand the causes of eating disorders, co-dependency, child sexual abuse and incest, the wounded child, dysfunctional families, the trauma of separation between parents and children due to the breakup of families and challenges of single-parenting. Ceres also encompasses the ancient knowledge of conscious dying and the psychological death and rebirth transformation process.

Pallas Athena, Goddess of Wisdom, refers to the dilemma of professional women who sacrifice relationship or children for career, sexism in the professional world, the wounds from the father-daughter interaction, androgyny, and taking responsibility for creating our reality. Pallas also provides insights into the causes of disease due to breakdown of the auto-immune system, and is a key to understanding learning disorders.

Vesta, the Temple Priestess, illuminates the need to reintegrate spiritual and sexual energies, focus on self-healing, find our vocation or meaningful work, and develop a deeper relationship with our own soul. Vesta symbolizes the importance of following a spiritual path to heal addictions and offers a clue to the spread of sexually-transmitted diseases.

Juno, the Goddess of Marriage, speaks to the redefinition of meaningful relationships, lesbian and gay couples, changing sexual roles, and the plight of powerless and battered women. Juno's story provides a foundation to understand the issues of projection, love addiction, dependency, domination, obsession, jealousy, betrayal, trust and power themes in relationships.

In addition, the asteroids help clarify and enhance the horoscope's existing astrological themes. It is not unusual for the asteroids to group around the major points of focus in the chart and complete major Aspect patterns.

© *Demetra George 1991, author of* Asteroid Goddesses

1995 ASTEROID EPHEMERIS

Reprinted with permission from Astro Communications Services, Inc.

1995	Ceres 1	Pallas 2	Juno 3	Vesta 4	1995	Sappho 80	Amor 1221	Pandora 55	Icarus 1566
JAN 1	19♎R44.5	05♉D58.9	10♐41.5	01♋R13.0	JAN 1	12♌R45.7	04♈29.6	19♐43.1	04≈12.3
JAN 11	18♎30.0	07♉08.0	13♐54.1	28♊48.2	11	10♌35.0	06♈34.2	23♐38.4	09≈47.3
JAN 21	16♎39.7	09♉12.3	17♐00.4	26♊53.0	21	07♌56.8	09♈01.0	27♐31.0	15≈56.9
JAN 31	14♎25.6	12♉03.3	19♐58.7	25♊37.9	31	05♌10.0	11♈46.8	01♑20.1	22≈52.0
FEB 10	12♎04.7	15♉33.7	22♐47.2	25♊07.8	FEB 10	02♌35.4	14♈48.5	05♑04.1	00♈49.1
FEB 20	09♎55.9	19♉36.2	25♐23.7	25♊D22.3	20	00♌30.6	18♈03.6	08♑41.7	10♈14.6
MAR 2	08♎14.7	24♉05.0	27♐46.3	26♊17.7	MAR 2	29♋06.3	21♈30.2	12♑11.5	21♈44.3
MAR 12	07♎11.9	28♉55.1	29♐52.0	27♊49.6	12	28♋27.1	25♈06.6	15♑31.4	01♉R15.6
MAR 22	06♎D52.1	04♊01.9	01♑38.1	29♊52.8	22	28♋D31.9	28♈51.3	18♑39.6	15♈44.7
APR 1	07♎14.9	09♊21.8	03♑01.5	02♋22.4	APR 1	29♋16.8	02♉43.4	21♑33.7	05♈30.3
APR 11	08♎17.6	14♊51.6	03♑58.7	05♋14.5	11	00♌36.9	06♉41.9	24♑10.9	01♈19.2
APR 21	09♎55.5	20♊28.5	04♑26.7	08♋25.2	21	02♌26.7	10♉46.1	26♑28.1	29≈13.3
MAY 1	12♎03.7	26♊05.8	04♑R26.7	11♋51.6	MAY 1	04♌41.4	14♉55.4	28♑21.8	27≈31.3
MAY 11	14♎37.7	01♋54.6	03♑45.2	15♋31.3	11	07♌16.8	19♉09.5	29♑47.9	25≈18.6
MAY 21	17♎33.3	07♋40.0	02♑34.6	19♋22.1	21	10♌09.1	23♉28.0	00≈42.7	21≈55.7
MAY 31	20♎47.0	13♋25.2	00♑54.3	23♋22.4	31	13♌15.5	27♉50.9	01≈02.4	16≈47.0
JUN 10	24♎15.8	19♋09.0	28♐51.1	27♋30.9	JUN 10	16♌33.4	02♊17.9	00≈R44.3	09≈27.3
JUN 20	27♎57.1	24♋50.1	26♐35.8	01♌46.2	20	20♌00.8	06♊49.0	29♑48.5	00≈04.7
JUN 30	01♏48.9	00♌28.2	24♐20.3	06♌07.6	30	23♌36.1	11♊24.5	28♑17.9	19♓40.5
JUL 10	05♏49.5	06♌02.7	22♐17.5	10♌34.3	JUL 10	27♌17.8	16♊04.2	26♑20.7	09♓55.9
JUL 20	09♏57.2	11♌33.0	20♐37.9	15♌05.4	20	01♍04.8	20♊48.6	24♑09.6	02♓10.0
JUL 30	14♏11.0	16♌58.9	19♐28.7	19♌40.6	30	04♍56.1	25♊38.1	21♑59.7	26♐45.9
AUG 9	18♏29.7	22♌20.2	18♐53.7	24♌19.2	AUG 9	08♍51.0	00♋32.6	20♑07.1	23♐30.1
AUG 19	22♏52.3	27♌36.6	18♐D53.5	29♌00.7	19	12♍48.4	05♋33.0	18♑44.0	21♐55.6
AUG 29	27♏18.1	02♍48.2	19♐26.8	03♍44.8	29	16♍48.0	10♋39.9	17♑58.3	21♐D37.9
SEP 8	01♐46.3	07♍54.5	20♐31.1	08♍30.8	SEP 8	20♍48.9	15♋53.6	17♑D53.9	22♐18.3
SEP 18	06♐16.1	12♍55.4	22♐03.2	13♍18.4	18	24♍50.4	21♋15.4	18♑29.9	23♐42.4
SEP 28	10♐47.0	17♍50.9	23♐59.9	18♍07.1	28	28♍52.1	26♋46.2	19♑43.9	25♐40.6
OCT 8	15♐18.1	22♍40.3	26♐18.3	22♍56.1	OCT 8	02♎53.2	02♌07.1	21♑32.3	28♐06.0
OCT 18	19♐48.7	27♍23.4	28♐55.5	27♍45.2	18	06♎52.8	08♌20.3	23♑50.9	00♑53.2
OCT 28	24♐18.1	01♎59.6	01♑49.1	02♎33.4	28	10♎50.4	14♌27.4	26♑35.7	03♑59.1
NOV 7	28♐45.5	06♎28.1	04♑57.0	07♎20.0	NOV 7	14♎44.8	20♌51.2	29♑43.3	07♑20.9
NOV 17	03♑10.1	10♎48.1	08♑17.2	12♎04.0	17	18♎35.1	27♌35.2	03≈10.1	10♑56.9
NOV 27	07♑30.9	14♎58.2	11♑48.1	16♎44.5	27	22♎20.0	04♍49.4	06≈53.6	14♑46.2
DEC 7	11♑46.7	18♎56.9	15♑28.2	21♎19.9	DEC 7	25♎58.2	12♍20.8	10≈51.3	18♑48.1
DEC 17	15♑56.6	22♎42.7	19♑16.1	25♎49.1	17	29♎28.0	20♍33.8	15≈00.9	23♑02.5
DEC 27	19♑59.1	26♎13.1	23♑10.9	00♏10.1	27	02♏47.6	29♍28.5	19≈20.7	27♑30.1
JAN 6	23♑52.5	29♎25.2	27♑11.3	04♏20.9	JAN 6	05♏54.5	09♎10.8	23≈49.1	02≈11.6

1995	Psyche 16	Eros 433	Lilith 1181	Toro 1685	1995	Diana 78	Hidalgo 944	Urania 30	Chiron 2060
JAN 1	29≈53.7	26♐58.2	01♏51.5	02≈42.4	JAN 1	12♏41.2	21♏17.6	26♋49.4	26♏20.1
JAN 11	04♓01.8	03♑18.2	06♏03.0	12≈31.4	11	16♏32.2	22♏13.8	29♋37.4	26♏R25.3
JAN 21	08♓18.0	09♑30.8	10♏19.7	23≈06.1	21	20♏06.4	23♏00.6	02♌03.3	26♏18.7
JAN 31	12♓41.0	15♑36.4	14♏40.6	04♓28.2	31	23♏21.3	23♏36.7	04♌03.3	26♏00.8
FEB 10	17♓09.4	21♑35.0	19♏04.9	16♓35.5	FEB 10	26♏13.3	24♏00.8	05♌32.8	25♏32.6
FEB 20	21♓42.1	27♑26.9	23♏31.9	29♓21.1	20	28♏39.1	24♏12.1	06♌27.6	24♏55.9
MAR 2	26♓18.1	03≈12.4	28♏00.8	12♈34.3	MAR 2	00♐34.7	24♏R09.7	06♌R17.7	24♏12.9
MAR 12	00♈56.3	08≈51.2	02♐30.9	26♈00.8	12	01♐55.7	23♏53.5	05♌10.2	23♏26.2
MAR 22	05♈35.9	14≈23.5	07♐01.5	09♉24.6	22	02♐38.2	23♏23.7	03♌24.7	22♏38.8
APR 1	10♈16.2	19≈49.4	11♐32.1	22♉30.9	APR 1	02♐R39.2	22♏41.1	01♌10.5	21♏53.4
APR 11	14♈56.4	25≈08.5	16♐01.8	05♊06.2	11	01♐57.4	21♏47.4	28♋41.8	21♏12.9
APR 21	19♈35.6	00♓20.2	20♐29.9	17♊00.6	21	00♐35.5	20♏44.8	26♋15.0	20♏39.6
MAY 1	24♈13.4	05♓24.8	24♐55.8	28♊09.9	MAY 1	28♏34.0	19♏36.2	24♋06.6	20♏15.3
MAY 11	28♈48.9	10♓21.0	29♐18.3	08♋30.1	11	26♏23.4	18♏24.8	22♋29.2	20♏01.4
MAY 21	03♉21.3	15♓08.3	03♑36.6	18♋05.8	21	24♏00.9	17♏14.1	21♋29.6	19♏D58.5
MAY 31	07♉50.0	19♓45.6	07♑49.5	27♋00.4	31	21♏48.5	16♏07.3	21♋D29.6	20♏06.7
JUN 10	12♉14.1	24♓10.8	11♑55.5	05♌18.6	JUN 10	20♏00.2	15♏07.6	21♋D10.9	20♏26.7
JUN 20	16♉32.5	28♓22.1	15♑53.0	13♌05.3	20	18♏45.2	14♏17.3	21♋31.5	20♏57.2
JUN 30	20♉44.5	02♈16.4	19♑40.1	20♌25.3	30	18♏07.5	13♏38.2	22♋28.4	21♏37.8
JUL 10	24♉48.4	05♈49.5	23♑14.0	27♌22.9	JUL 10	18♏D07.8	13♏11.5	23♋57.8	22♏27.6
JUL 20	28♉43.2	08♈56.5	26♑32.0	04♍01.3	20	18♏43.5	12♏57.6	25♋55.1	23♏25.7
JUL 30	02♊07.0	11♈29.7	29♑34.1	10♍24.0	30	19♏51.1	12♏D56.7	28♋16.7	24♏31.2
AUG 9	05♊57.7	13♈19.8	02≈04.6	16♍33.3	AUG 9	21♏26.8	13♏08.3	00♍59.1	25♏43.0
AUG 19	09♊13.1	14♈35.8	04≈10.0	22♍31.4	19	23♏26.4	13♏31.6	03♍59.1	26♏59.9
AUG 29	12♊10.3	14♈R03.7	05≈40.7	28♍20.3	29	25♏46.4	14♏05.7	07♍14.4	28♏21.1
SEP 8	14♊45.8	12♈31.9	06≈31.0	04♎01.3	SEP 8	28♏23.6	14♏49.6	10♍42.8	29♏45.5
SEP 18	16♊56.0	09♈37.2	06≈R36.6	09♎35.6	18	01♐15.5	15♏42.1	14♍22.4	01♐11.8
SEP 28	18♊36.5	05♈32.4	05≈55.0	15♎04.5	28	04♐19.4	16♏42.0	18♍11.7	02♐39.1
OCT 8	19♊42.7	00♈56.7	04≈29.7	20♎28.6	OCT 8	07♐33.5	17♏48.0	22♍09.5	04♐06.3
OCT 18	20♊10.9	26♓43.7	02≈31.0	25♎48.7	18	10♐55.8	18♏58.8	26♍14.4	05♐32.2
OCT 28	19♊R57.9	23♓41.4	00≈16.0	01♏05.3	28	14♐25.0	20♏13.3	00♎25.6	06♐55.7
NOV 7	19♊03.8	22♓17.8	28♑06.9	06♏18.9	NOV 7	17♐59.8	21♏30.1	04♎42.1	08♐15.5
NOV 17	17♊32.7	22♓D33.5	26♑24.3	11♏29.8	17	21♐38.7	22♏48.0	09♎03.1	09♐30.5
NOV 27	15♊33.7	24♓22.1	25♑23.3	16♏38.4	27	25♐20.8	24♏05.5	13♎27.9	10♐39.4
DEC 7	13♊21.4	27♓30.2	25♑D12.0	21♏44.7	DEC 7	29♐05.0	25♏21.4	17♎55.5	11♐40.8
DEC 17	11♊12.4	01♈44.3	25♑50.8	26♏48.9	17	02♑53.0	26♏34.3	22♎23.0	12♐33.8
DEC 27	09♊22.9	06♈54.1	27♑16.5	01♐51.1	27	06♑35.5	27♏42.8	26♎56.7	13♐17.0
JAN 6	08♊05.0	12♈51.0	29♑23.9	06♐51.2	JAN 6	10♑19.8	28♏45.6	01♏28.7	13♐49.6

NOON EPHEMERIS: GMT*

JANUARY 1995

Day	☉	Noon ☽	True ☊	☿	♀	♂	♃	♄	♅	♆	♇
1 Su	10♑35 59	11♑13 7	13♏12.5	21♑14.4	24♏18.9	2♍39.4	4♐49.9	8♓ 1.9	25♑30.1	22♑35.2	29♏32.3
2 M	11 37 10	25 58 4	13R 3.1	22 51.6	25 14.3	2R 40.1	5 1.9	8 7.0	25 33.5	22 37.4	29 34.2
3 Tu	12 38 21	10♒23 43	12 53.2	24 28.8	26 10.3	2 40.0	5 13.8	8 12.1	25 37.0	22 39.7	29 36.1
4 W	13 39 32	24 24 14	12 44.0	26 5.8	27 6.8	2 39.1	5 25.7	8 17.3	25 40.5	22 41.9	29 38.0
5 Th	14 40 43	7♓56 48	12 36.4	27 42.5	28 3.9	2 37.5	5 37.4	8 22.6	25 44.0	22 44.2	29 39.8
6 F	15 41 53	21 1 32	12 31.1	29 18.9	29 1.6	2 35.1	5 49.2	8 28.0	25 47.5	22 46.5	29 41.7
7 Sa	16 43 3	3♈40 58	12 28.1	0♒54.7	29 59.7	2 31.8	6 0.8	8 33.4	25 51.0	22 48.7	29 43.5
8 Su	17 44 12	15 59 18	12D 27.1	2 29.9	0♐58.3	2 27.8	6 12.4	8 38.8	25 54.5	22 51.0	29 45.3
9 M	18 45 21	28 1 40	12 27.3	4 4.2	1 57.4	2 23.0	6 23.9	8 44.4	25 58.0	22 53.3	29 47.0
10 Tu	19 46 29	9♉53 39	12R 27.7	5 37.3	2 57.0	2 17.4	6 35.3	8 50.0	26 1.6	22 55.5	29 48.7
11 W	20 47 37	21 40 40	12 27.3	7 9.0	3 57.0	2 10.9	6 46.6	8 55.7	26 5.1	22 57.8	29 50.4
12 Th	21 48 45	3♊27 45	12 25.0	8 39.0	4 57.4	2 3.7	6 57.9	9 1.4	26 8.6	23 0.1	29 52.1
13 F	22 49 52	15 19 17	12 20.2	10 6.9	5 58.3	1 55.7	7 9.1	9 7.2	26 12.2	23 2.4	29 53.8
14 Sa	23 50 58	27 18 46	12 12.5	11 32.1	6 59.5	1 46.8	7 20.2	9 13.0	26 15.7	23 4.7	29 55.4
15 Su	24 52 4	9♋28 44	12 2.1	12 54.3	8 1.1	1 37.2	7 31.2	9 18.9	26 19.3	23 6.9	29 57.0
16 M	25 53 10	21 50 44	11 49.6	14 12.9	9 3.1	1 26.7	7 42.2	9 24.9	26 22.8	23 9.2	29 58.6
17 Tu	26 54 15	4♌25 19	11 36.0	15 27.2	10 5.5	1 15.5	7 53.0	9 30.9	26 26.4	23 11.5	0♐ 0.1
18 W	27 55 19	17 12 21	11 22.6	16 36.5	11 8.2	1 3.5	8 3.8	9 37.0	26 29.9	23 13.8	0 1.6
19 Th	28 56 23	0♍11 13	11 10.5	17 40.1	12 11.2	0 50.7	8 14.5	9 43.2	26 33.4	23 16.0	0 3.1
20 F	29 57 26	13 21 12	11 0.8	18 37.1	13 14.6	0 37.1	8 25.1	9 49.3	26 37.0	23 18.3	0 4.6
21 Sa	0♒58 29	26 41 50	10 54.1	19 26.7	14 18.3	0 22.8	8 35.6	9 55.6	26 40.5	23 20.6	0 6.0
22 Su	1 59 32	10♎13 5	10 50.4	20 8.0	15 22.3	0 7.7	8 46.0	10 1.9	26 44.1	23 22.8	0 7.4
23 M	3 0 34	23 55 23	10 49.1	20 40.2	16 26.5	29♌51.9	8 56.3	10 8.2	26 47.6	23 25.1	0 8.8
24 Tu	4 1 35	7♏49 18	10 49.0	21 2.5	17 31.1	29 35.3	9 6.5	10 14.6	26 51.1	23 27.3	0 10.1
25 W	5 2 37	21 55 10	10 48.8	21 14.2	18 35.9	29 18.1	9 16.7	10 21.0	26 54.6	23 29.6	0 11.4
26 Th	6 3 38	6♐12 29	10 47.1	21R 14.7	19 41.0	29 0.2	9 26.7	10 27.5	26 58.2	23 31.8	0 12.7
27 F	7 4 38	20 39 15	10 42.9	21 3.9	20 46.4	28 41.7	9 36.6	10 34.0	27 1.7	23 34.0	0 13.9
28 Sa	8 5 38	5♑11 37	10 35.6	20 41.7	21 52.0	28 22.5	9 46.4	10 40.6	27 5.2	23 36.3	0 15.2
29 Su	9 6 37	19 44 0	10 25.6	20 8.4	22 57.8	28 2.7	9 56.1	10 47.2	27 8.7	23 38.5	0 16.3
30 M	10 7 35	4♒ 9 39	10 13.6	19 24.6	24 3.8	27 42.4	10 5.7	10 53.9	27 12.2	23 40.7	0 17.5
31 Tu	11 8 32	18 21 43	10 0.9	18 31.6	25 10.1	27 21.5	10 15.2	11 0.6	27 15.6	23 42.9	0 18.6

LONGITUDE

FEBRUARY 1995

Day	☉	Noon ☽	True ☊	☿	♀	♂	♃	♄	♅	♆	♇
1 W	12♒ 9 28	2♓14 25	9♏48.6	17♒30.7	26♐16.5	27♌ 0.2	10♐24.6	11♓ 7.3	27♑19.1	23♑45.1	0♐19.7
2 Th	13 10 22	15 43 59	9R 38.1	16R 23.7	27 23.2	26R 38.4	10 33.9	11 14.1	27 22.5	23 47.3	0 20.7
3 F	14 11 16	28 49 2	9 30.1	15 12.6	28 30.0	26 16.1	10 43.0	11 20.9	27 26.0	23 49.4	0 21.8
4 Sa	15 12 8	11♈30 36	9 24.9	13 59.4	29 37.1	25 53.6	10 52.1	11 27.8	27 29.4	23 51.6	0 22.7
5 Su	16 12 59	23 51 36	9 22.3	12 46.4	0♑44.3	25 30.6	11 1.0	11 34.6	27 32.8	23 53.7	0 23.7
6 M	17 13 48	5♉56 24	9 21.4	11 35.3	1 51.7	25 7.5	11 9.8	11 41.6	27 36.2	23 55.9	0 24.6
7 Tu	18 14 36	17 50 12	9 21.4	10 28.1	2 59.2	24 44.0	11 18.4	11 48.5	27 39.6	23 58.0	0 25.5
8 W	19 15 23	29 38 34	9 20.9	9 26.1	4 6.9	24 20.4	11 27.0	11 55.5	27 43.0	24 0.1	0 26.3
9 Th	20 16 8	11♊27 5	9 19.1	8 30.5	5 14.8	23 56.6	11 35.4	12 2.5	27 46.3	24 2.2	0 27.2
10 F	21 16 51	23 20 58	9 15.0	7 42.2	6 22.8	23 32.7	11 43.7	12 9.5	27 49.6	24 4.3	0 27.9
11 Sa	22 17 33	5♋24 45	9 8.2	7 1.6	7 31.0	23 8.8	11 51.9	12 16.6	27 53.0	24 6.4	0 28.7
12 Su	23 18 14	17 42 2	8 58.8	6 29.0	8 39.4	22 44.8	11 59.9	12 23.7	27 56.3	24 8.4	0 29.4
13 M	24 18 53	0♌15 15	8 47.2	6 4.5	9 47.8	22 20.9	12 7.8	12 30.8	27 59.5	24 10.5	0 30.1
14 Tu	25 19 30	13 5 26	8 34.4	5 48.0	10 56.4	21 57.0	12 15.6	12 37.9	28 2.8	24 12.5	0 30.7
15 W	26 20 6	26 12 14	8 21.5	5 39.1	12 5.2	21 33.3	12 23.3	12 45.1	28 6.0	24 14.5	0 31.3
16 Th	27 20 40	9♍34 7	8 9.8	5D 37.6	13 14.1	21 9.7	12 30.8	12 52.3	28 9.2	24 16.5	0 31.9
17 F	28 21 13	23 8 40	8 0.3	5 43.0	14 23.1	20 46.3	12 38.1	12 59.5	28 12.4	24 18.5	0 32.4
18 Sa	29 21 44	6♎53 11	7 53.6	5 54.9	15 32.2	20 23.2	12 45.4	13 6.7	28 15.6	24 20.4	0 32.9
19 Su	0♓22 14	20 45 8	7 50.0	6 13.0	16 41.4	20 0.4	12 52.5	13 13.9	28 18.7	24 22.3	0 33.4
20 M	1 22 43	4♏42 33	7D 48.8	6 36.7	17 50.8	19 37.9	12 59.4	13 21.2	28 21.9	24 24.3	0 33.8
21 Tu	2 23 10	18 44 3	7 49.0	7 5.7	19 0.3	19 15.8	13 6.2	13 28.4	28 24.9	24 26.2	0 34.2
22 W	3 23 37	2♐48 47	7R 49.5	7 39.6	20 9.9	18 54.0	13 12.9	13 35.7	28 28.0	24 28.0	0 34.6
23 Th	4 24 2	16 55 59	7 48.9	8 17.9	21 19.6	18 32.7	13 19.4	13 43.0	28 31.1	24 29.9	0 34.9
24 F	5 24 25	1♑ 4 28	7 46.3	9 0.4	22 29.4	18 11.9	13 25.8	13 50.3	28 34.1	24 31.8	0 35.2
25 Sa	6 24 48	15 12 22	7 41.2	9 46.8	23 39.3	17 51.6	13 32.0	13 57.7	28 37.1	24 33.6	0 35.5
26 Su	7 25 8	29 16 51	7 33.6	10 36.7	24 49.3	17 31.9	13 38.0	14 5.0	28 40.0	24 35.4	0 35.7
27 M	8 25 28	13♒14 17	7 24.2	11 29.9	25 59.4	17 12.7	13 43.9	14 12.3	28 43.0	24 37.2	0 35.9
28 Tu	9 25 45	27 0 41	7 13.9	12 26.1	27 9.6	16 54.2	13 49.7	14 19.7	28 45.9	24 38.9	0 36.0

Ephemeris reprinted with permission from Astro Communications Services, Inc.

*Giving the positions of planets daily at noon, in LONGITUDE Greenwich Mean Time

NOON EPHEMERIS: GMT* — MARCH 1995

Day	☉	Noon ☽	True ☊	☿	♀	♂	♃	♄	♅	♆	♇
1 W	10♓26 1	10♓32 19	7♏ 4.0	13♒25.2	28♑19.8	16♌36.2	13♐55.3	14♓27.0	28♑48.8	24♑40.7	0♐36.1
2 Th	11 26 15	23 46 22	6R 55.4	14 26.9	29 30.2	16R 19.0	14 0.7	14 34.4	28 51.6	24 42.4	0 36.2
3 F	12 26 27	6♈41 23	6 48.9	15 31.1	0♒40.6	16 2.4	14 5.9	14 41.8	28 54.4	24 44.1	0R 36.2
4 Sa	13 26 38	19 17 32	6 44.9	16 37.6	1 51.0	15 46.5	14 11.0	14 49.1	28 57.2	24 45.7	0 36.2
5 Su	14 26 46	1♉36 29	6D 43.1	17 46.3	3 1.6	15 31.4	14 16.0	14 56.5	28 59.9	24 47.4	0 36.2
6 M	15 26 52	13 41 19	6 43.1	18 57.0	4 12.2	15 17.0	14 20.7	15 3.9	29 2.7	24 49.0	0 36.1
7 Tu	16 26 57	25 36 5	6 44.1	20 9.7	5 22.9	15 3.3	14 25.3	15 11.3	29 5.3	24 50.6	0 36.0
8 W	17 26 59	7♊25 36	6 45.3	21 24.2	6 33.7	14 50.4	14 29.8	15 18.6	29 8.0	24 52.1	0 35.9
9 Th	18 26 59	19 15 4	6R 45.8	22 40.5	7 44.5	14 38.3	14 34.0	15 26.0	29 10.6	24 53.7	0 35.7
10 F	19 26 57	1♋ 9 47	6 44.9	23 58.5	8 55.4	14 26.9	14 38.1	15 33.4	29 13.2	24 55.2	0 35.5
11 Sa	20 26 52	13 14 50	6 42.2	25 18.1	10 6.3	14 16.3	14 42.1	15 40.7	29 15.7	24 56.7	0 35.3
12 Su	21 26 46	25 34 42	6 37.6	26 39.2	11 17.3	14 6.5	14 45.8	15 48.1	29 18.2	24 58.2	0 35.0
13 M	22 26 37	8♌13 0	6 31.4	28 1.9	12 28.4	13 57.6	14 49.4	15 55.4	29 20.7	24 59.6	0 34.7
14 Tu	23 26 26	21 11 56	6 24.2	29 26.0	13 39.5	13 49.3	14 52.8	16 2.7	29 23.1	25 1.0	0 34.4
15 W	24 26 13	4♍32 11	6 16.7	0♓51.5	14 50.6	13 41.9	14 56.0	16 10.1	29 25.5	25 2.4	0 34.0
16 Th	25 25 58	18 12 35	6 9.8	2 18.5	16 1.9	13 35.3	14 59.1	16 17.4	29 27.9	25 3.7	0 33.6
17 F	26 25 41	2♎10 19	6 4.3	3 46.8	17 13.1	13 29.4	15 1.9	16 24.7	29 30.2	25 5.1	0 33.2
18 Sa	27 25 22	16 21 15	6 0.7	5 16.5	18 24.5	13 24.4	15 4.6	16 32.0	29 32.5	25 6.4	0 32.7
19 Su	28 25 1	0♏40 35	5D 59.1	6 47.5	19 35.8	13 20.1	15 7.1	16 39.2	29 34.7	25 7.6	0 32.2
20 M	29 24 38	15 3 29	5 59.2	8 19.9	20 47.3	13 16.5	15 9.5	16 46.5	29 36.9	25 8.9	0 31.6
21 Tu	0♈24 14	29 25 44	6 0.4	9 53.5	21 58.8	13 13.7	15 11.6	16 53.8	29 39.1	25 10.1	0 31.1
22 W	1 23 48	13♐43 55	6 1.9	11 28.5	23 10.3	13 11.7	15 13.6	17 1.0	29 41.2	25 11.3	0 30.5
23 Th	2 23 20	27 55 38	6R 3.0	13 4.8	24 21.9	13 10.5	15 15.4	17 8.2	29 43.3	25 12.5	0 29.8
24 F	3 22 50	11♑59 7	6 2.9	14 42.4	25 33.5	13D 9.9	15 17.0	17 15.4	29 45.3	25 13.6	0 29.2
25 Sa	4 22 19	25 53 9	6 1.3	16 21.3	26 45.2	13 10.1	15 18.4	17 22.6	29 47.3	25 14.7	0 28.5
26 Su	5 21 46	9♒36 40	5 58.2	18 1.5	27 56.9	13 11.1	15 19.6	17 29.7	29 49.2	25 15.8	0 27.8
27 M	6 21 11	23 8 40	5 54.1	19 43.0	29 8.6	13 12.7	15 20.7	17 36.8	29 51.1	25 16.8	0 27.0
28 Tu	7 20 34	6♓28 8	5 49.4	21 25.9	0♓20.4	13 15.1	15 21.5	17 44.0	29 53.0	25 17.8	0 26.2
29 W	8 19 55	19 34 7	5 44.8	23 10.2	1 32.3	13 18.1	15 22.2	17 51.0	29 54.8	25 18.8	0 25.4
30 Th	9 19 14	2♈26 0	5 41.0	24 55.7	2 44.1	13 21.9	15 22.6	17 58.1	29 56.6	25 19.7	0 24.5
31 F	10 18 32	15 3 35	5 38.2	26 42.7	3 56.0	13 26.3	15 22.9	18 5.1	29 58.3	25 20.6	0 23.7

LONGITUDE — APRIL 1995

Day	☉	Noon ☽	True ☊	☿	♀	♂	♃	♄	♅	♆	♇
1 Sa	11♈17 47	27♈27 24	5♏36.8	28♓31.0	5♓ 7.9	13♌31.4	15♐23.0	18♓12.1	29♑60.0	25♑21.5	0♐22.8
2 Su	12 17 0	9♉38 41	5D 36.7	0♈20.7	6 19.9	13 37.2	15R 22.9	18 19.1	0♒ 1.6	25 22.4	0R 21.8
3 M	13 16 11	21 39 34	5 37.6	2 11.8	7 31.8	13 43.6	15 22.6	18 26.0	0 3.2	25 23.2	0 20.9
4 Tu	14 15 20	3♊32 55	5 39.1	4 4.3	8 43.8	13 50.7	15 22.2	18 32.9	0 4.8	25 24.0	0 19.9
5 W	15 14 26	15 22 20	5 40.8	5 58.2	9 55.9	13 58.4	15 21.5	18 39.8	0 6.3	25 24.7	0 18.9
6 Th	16 13 31	27 12 0	5 42.4	7 53.5	11 7.9	14 6.7	15 20.7	18 46.7	0 7.7	25 25.4	0 17.8
7 F	17 12 33	9♋ 6 30	5 43.3	9 50.2	12 20.0	14 15.6	15 19.6	18 53.5	0 9.1	25 26.1	0 16.8
8 Sa	18 11 33	21 10 39	5R 43.6	11 48.3	13 32.1	14 25.1	15 18.4	19 0.2	0 10.5	25 26.8	0 15.7
9 Su	19 10 30	3♌29 8	5 43.0	13 47.7	14 44.2	14 35.1	15 17.0	19 7.0	0 11.8	25 27.4	0 14.6
10 M	20 9 25	16 6 18	5 41.7	15 48.3	15 56.3	14 45.8	15 15.4	19 13.7	0 13.0	25 28.0	0 13.4
11 Tu	21 8 18	29 5 36	5 40.0	17 50.2	17 8.5	14 57.0	15 13.7	19 20.3	0 14.2	25 28.6	0 12.3
12 W	22 7 9	12♍29 11	5 38.1	19 53.3	18 20.7	15 8.7	15 11.7	19 26.9	0 15.4	25 29.1	0 11.1
13 Th	23 5 57	26 17 26	5 36.4	21 57.4	19 32.9	15 21.0	15 9.6	19 33.5	0 16.5	25 29.6	0 9.9
14 F	24 4 43	10♎28 36	5 35.1	24 2.5	20 45.1	15 33.7	15 7.2	19 40.1	0 17.6	25 30.0	0 8.6
15 Sa	25 3 27	24 58 46	5 34.4	26 8.3	21 57.4	15 47.0	15 4.7	19 46.6	0 18.6	25 30.5	0 7.4
16 Su	26 2 10	9♏42 7	5D 34.3	28 14.8	23 9.7	16 0.8	15 2.1	19 53.0	0 19.6	25 30.9	0 6.1
17 M	27 0 50	24 31 36	5 34.7	0♉21.7	24 22.0	16 15.1	14 59.2	19 59.4	0 20.5	25 31.2	0 4.8
18 Tu	27 59 29	9♐19 58	5 35.4	2 28.8	25 34.3	16 29.8	14 56.2	20 5.8	0 21.3	25 31.5	0 3.5
19 W	28 58 6	24 0 35	5 36.1	4 35.8	26 46.6	16 45.0	14 53.0	20 12.1	0 22.2	25 31.8	0 2.1
20 Th	29 56 41	8♑28 12	5 36.6	6 42.5	27 59.0	17 0.7	14 49.6	20 18.4	0 22.9	25 32.1	0 0.8
21 F	0♉55 15	22 39 20	5 36.9	8 48.6	29 11.4	17 16.8	14 46.1	20 24.6	0 23.7	25 32.3	29♏59.4
22 Sa	1 53 47	6♒32 11	5R 36.9	10 53.7	0♈23.8	17 33.3	14 42.4	20 30.7	0 24.3	25 32.5	29 58.0
23 Su	2 52 17	20 6 24	5 36.7	12 57.6	1 36.2	17 50.3	14 38.5	20 36.9	0 25.0	25 32.7	29 56.6
24 M	3 50 46	3♓22 40	5 36.5	14 59.9	2 48.7	18 7.7	14 34.4	20 42.9	0 25.5	25 32.8	29 55.2
25 Tu	4 49 13	16 22 17	5 36.2	17 0.2	4 1.1	18 25.5	14 30.2	20 48.9	0 26.0	25 32.9	29 53.7
26 W	5 47 38	29 6 52	5D 36.1	18 58.4	5 13.6	18 43.7	14 25.8	20 54.9	0 26.5	25 33.0	29 52.3
27 Th	6 46 2	11♈38 5	5 36.1	20 54.0	6 26.1	19 2.3	14 21.3	21 0.8	0 26.9	25R 33.0	29 50.8
28 F	7 44 24	23 57 39	5 36.2	22 47.0	7 38.6	19 21.4	14 16.6	21 6.7	0 27.3	25 33.0	29 49.3
29 Sa	8 42 45	6♉ 7 13	5R 36.3	24 36.9	8 51.1	19 40.7	14 11.7	21 12.4	0 27.6	25 33.0	29 47.8
30 Su	9 41 3	18 8 30	5 36.3	26 23.6	10 3.7	20 0.5	14 6.7	21 18.2	0 27.9	25 32.9	29 46.3

*Giving the positions of planets daily at noon, in LONGITUDE Greenwich Mean Time

NOON EPHEMERIS: GMT* — MAY 1995

Day	☉	Noon ☽	True ☊	☿	♀	♂	♃	♄	♅	♆	♇
1 M	10♉39 20	0♊ 3 25	5♏36.0	28♉ 6.9	11♈16.2	20♌20.6	14♐ 1.6	21♓23.9	0♒28.1	25♑32.8	29♏44.7
2 Tu	11 37 35	11 54 6	5R35.5	29 46.6	12 28.8	20 41.1	13R56.3	21 29.5	0 28.3	25R32.7	29R43.2
3 W	12 35 48	23 43 7	5 34.7	1♊22.6	13 41.3	21 2.0	13 50.9	21 35.0	0 28.4	25 32.5	29 41.6
4 Th	13 33 59	5♋33 27	5 33.7	2 54.8	14 53.9	21 23.2	13 45.3	21 40.5	0 28.4	25 32.3	29 40.1
5 F	14 32 8	17 28 31	5 32.7	4 23.1	16 6.5	21 44.7	13 39.6	21 45.9	0R28.5	25 32.1	29 38.5
6 Sa	15 30 16	29 32 13	5 31.8	5 47.4	17 19.1	22 6.5	13 33.8	21 51.3	0 28.4	25 31.8	29 36.9
7 Su	16 28 21	11♌48 41	5 31.2	7 7.5	18 31.7	22 28.7	13 27.8	21 56.6	0 28.3	25 31.5	29 35.3
8 M	17 26 25	24 22 10	5D31.1	8 23.5	19 44.3	22 51.2	13 21.7	22 1.8	0 28.2	25 31.2	29 33.7
9 Tu	18 24 26	7♍16 41	5 31.6	9 35.2	20 56.9	23 14.0	13 15.5	22 7.0	0 28.0	25 30.9	29 32.1
10 W	19 22 26	20 35 31	5 32.4	10 42.6	22 9.6	23 37.1	13 9.2	22 12.1	0 27.8	25 30.5	29 30.5
11 Th	20 20 23	4♎20 44	5 33.4	11 45.7	23 22.2	24 0.5	13 2.8	22 17.1	0 27.5	25 30.1	29 28.8
12 F	21 18 19	18 32 28	5 34.3	12 44.3	24 34.8	24 24.1	12 56.3	22 22.1	0 27.2	25 29.6	29 27.2
13 Sa	22 16 14	3♏ 8 26	5R34.8	13 38.4	25 47.5	24 48.1	12 49.7	22 27.0	0 26.8	25 29.1	29 25.5
14 Su	23 14 6	18 3 37	5 34.6	14 27.9	27 0.2	25 12.3	12 43.0	22 31.8	0 26.4	25 28.6	29 23.9
15 M	24 11 57	3♐10 28	5 33.5	15 12.8	28 12.9	25 36.8	12 36.2	22 36.5	0 25.9	25 28.1	29 22.3
16 Tu	25 9 47	18 19 49	5 31.7	15 53.0	29 25.6	26 1.5	12 29.3	22 41.2	0 25.4	25 27.5	29 20.6
17 W	26 7 36	3♑22 13	5 29.2	16 28.4	0♉38.3	26 26.5	12 22.3	22 45.8	0 24.8	25 26.9	29 19.0
18 Th	27 5 23	18 9 17	5 26.7	16 59.1	1 51.0	26 51.8	12 15.2	22 50.3	0 24.2	25 26.3	29 17.3
19 F	28 3 9	2♒34 56	5 24.4	17 25.0	3 3.7	27 17.3	12 8.1	22 54.8	0 23.5	25 25.6	29 15.6
20 Sa	29 0 54	16 35 49	5 22.8	17 46.0	4 16.5	27 43.1	12 0.9	22 59.2	0 22.8	25 24.9	29 14.0
21 Su	29 58 38	0♓11 13	5D22.2	18 2.1	5 29.3	28 9.0	11 53.6	23 3.5	0 22.1	25 24.2	29 12.3
22 M	0♊56 20	13 22 27	5 22.6	18 13.4	6 42.0	28 35.3	11 46.3	23 7.7	0 21.3	25 23.5	29 10.7
23 Tu	1 54 2	26 12 14	5 23.7	18 19.9	7 54.8	29 1.7	11 38.9	23 11.8	0 20.4	25 22.7	29 9.0
24 W	2 51 43	8♈43 58	5 25.3	18R21.7	9 7.6	29 28.4	11 31.4	23 15.9	0 19.5	25 21.9	29 7.3
25 Th	3 49 22	21 1 14	5 26.8	18 18.8	10 20.5	29 55.3	11 23.9	23 19.9	0 18.6	25 21.1	29 5.7
26 F	4 47 1	3♉ 7 30	5R27.5	18 11.5	11 33.3	0♍22.4	11 16.4	23 23.8	0 17.6	25 20.2	29 4.0
27 Sa	5 44 38	15 5 49	5 27.2	17 59.8	12 46.1	0 49.8	11 8.9	23 27.6	0 16.5	25 19.3	29 2.4
28 Su	6 42 15	26 58 54	5 25.4	17 44.1	13 59.0	1 17.4	11 1.3	23 31.3	0 15.5	25 18.4	29 0.7
29 M	7 39 50	8♊49 1	5 22.0	17 24.7	15 11.8	1 45.1	10 53.7	23 35.0	0 14.4	25 17.5	28 59.1
30 Tu	8 37 24	20 38 14	5 17.2	17 1.8	16 24.7	2 13.1	10 46.0	23 38.5	0 13.2	25 16.5	28 57.5
31 W	9 34 57	2♋28 30	5 11.4	16 36.0	17 37.6	2 41.3	10 38.4	23 42.0	0 12.0	25 15.5	28 55.8

LONGITUDE — JUNE 1995

Day	☉	Noon ☽	True ☊	☿	♀	♂	♃	♄	♅	♆	♇
1 Th	10♊32 29	14♋21 50	5♏ 5.1	16♊ 7.5	18♉50.5	3♍ 9.7	10♐30.7	23♓45.4	0♒10.7	25♑14.5	28♏54.2
2 F	11 30 0	26 20 29	4R58.8	15R37.0	20 3.4	3 38.3	10R23.1	23 48.7	0R 9.5	25R13.5	28R52.6
3 Sa	12 27 29	8♌27 7	4 53.5	15 4.9	21 16.3	4 7.1	10 15.5	23 51.9	0 8.1	25 12.4	28 51.0
4 Su	13 24 58	20 44 46	4 49.4	14 31.8	22 29.2	4 36.0	10 7.8	23 55.0	0 6.8	25 11.4	28 49.4
5 M	14 22 25	3♍16 54	4 47.0	13 58.3	23 42.1	5 5.2	10 0.2	23 58.1	0 5.4	25 10.3	28 47.8
6 Tu	15 19 50	16 7 10	4D46.3	13 24.9	24 55.1	5 34.5	9 52.6	24 1.0	0 3.9	25 9.1	28 46.3
7 W	16 17 15	29 19 10	4 46.9	12 52.2	26 8.0	6 4.0	9 45.0	24 3.9	0 2.4	25 8.0	28 44.7
8 Th	17 14 38	12♎55 52	4 48.1	12 20.7	27 21.0	6 33.7	9 37.5	24 6.6	0 0.9	25 6.8	28 43.1
9 F	18 12 0	26 59 0	4 49.1	11 51.1	28 33.9	7 3.5	9 30.0	24 9.3	29♑59.3	25 5.6	28 41.6
10 Sa	19 9 22	11♏28 12	4R49.1	11 23.8	29 46.9	7 33.5	9 22.5	24 11.9	29 57.7	25 4.4	28 40.1
11 Su	20 6 42	26 20 22	4 47.5	10 59.2	0♊59.9	8 3.7	9 15.1	24 14.4	29 56.1	25 3.1	28 38.5
12 M	21 4 2	11♐29 16	4 43.9	10 37.8	2 12.9	8 34.1	9 7.8	24 16.8	29 54.4	25 1.9	28 37.0
13 Tu	22 1 20	26 45 53	4 38.4	10 19.9	3 25.9	9 4.5	9 0.5	24 19.1	29 52.7	25 0.6	28 35.6
14 W	22 58 38	11♑59 35	4 31.7	10 5.9	4 38.9	9 35.2	8 53.2	24 21.3	29 51.0	24 59.3	28 34.1
15 Th	23 55 56	26 59 57	4 24.6	9 55.9	5 52.0	10 6.0	8 46.0	24 23.4	29 49.2	24 58.0	28 32.6
16 F	24 53 13	11♒38 27	4 18.0	9 50.2	7 5.0	10 37.0	8 38.9	24 25.4	29 47.4	24 56.7	28 31.2
17 Sa	25 50 29	25 49 44	4 12.8	9D48.9	8 18.1	11 8.1	8 31.9	24 27.3	29 45.6	24 55.3	28 29.7
18 Su	26 47 46	9♓31 46	4 9.3	9 52.1	9 31.2	11 39.3	8 24.9	24 29.2	29 43.7	24 54.0	28 28.3
19 M	27 45 2	22 45 28	4D 7.8	9 59.9	10 44.3	12 10.7	8 18.1	24 30.9	29 41.8	24 52.6	28 26.9
20 Tu	28 42 17	5♈33 52	4 7.8	10 12.4	11 57.4	12 42.3	8 11.3	24 32.5	29 39.9	24 51.2	28 25.6
21 W	29 39 33	18 1 15	4 8.7	10 29.5	13 10.6	13 14.0	8 4.6	24 34.1	29 38.0	24 49.8	28 24.2
22 Th	0♋36 48	0♉12 22	4R 9.5	10 51.3	14 23.8	13 45.8	7 58.0	24 35.5	29 36.0	24 48.3	28 22.9
23 F	1 34 3	12 11 56	4 9.3	11 17.7	15 36.9	14 17.8	7 51.5	24 36.8	29 34.0	24 46.9	28 21.5
24 Sa	2 31 18	24 4 17	4 7.3	11 48.7	16 50.1	14 49.9	7 45.1	24 38.1	29 31.9	24 45.4	28 20.2
25 Su	3 28 33	5♊53 10	4 2.9	12 24.2	18 3.3	15 22.1	7 38.9	24 39.2	29 29.9	24 43.9	28 19.0
26 M	4 25 48	17 41 41	3 56.0	13 4.1	19 16.6	15 54.5	7 32.7	24 40.3	29 27.8	24 42.5	28 17.7
27 Tu	5 23 2	29 32 13	3 46.8	13 48.5	20 29.8	16 27.1	7 26.7	24 41.2	29 25.7	24 41.0	28 16.5
28 W	6 20 17	11♋26 40	3 35.9	14 37.2	21 43.1	16 59.7	7 20.7	24 42.0	29 23.6	24 39.5	28 15.3
29 Th	7 17 31	23 26 32	3 24.2	15 30.2	22 56.4	17 32.5	7 14.9	24 42.8	29 21.4	24 37.9	28 14.1
30 F	8 14 44	5♌33 11	3 12.6	16 27.4	24 9.7	18 5.5	7 9.3	24 43.4	29 19.2	24 36.4	28 12.9

*Giving the positions of planets daily at noon, in LONGITUDE Greenwich Mean Time

NOON EPHEMERIS: GMT* JULY 1995

Day	☉	Noon ☽	True ☊	☿	♀	♂	♃	♄	♅	♆	♇
1 Sa	9♋11 58	17♌48 3	3♏ 2.3	17♊28.8	25♊23.0	18♍38.5	7♐ 3.8	24♓44.0	29♑17.0	24♑34.9	28♏11.7
2 Su	10 9 11	0♍12 53	2R 54.0	18 34.3	26 36.3	19 11.7	6R 58.4	24 44.4	29R 14.8	24R 33.3	28R 10.6
3 M	11 6 24	12 49 52	2 48.4	19 43.8	27 49.6	19 45.0	6 53.1	24 44.7	29 12.6	24 31.7	28 9.5
4 Tu	12 3 36	25 41 37	2 45.3	20 57.4	29 3.0	20 18.4	6 48.0	24 45.0	29 10.3	24 30.2	28 8.4
5 W	13 0 48	8♎51 2	2D 44.3	22 14.9	0♋16.4	20 52.0	6 43.1	24 45.1	29 8.1	24 28.6	28 7.4
6 Th	13 58 0	22 21 0	2 44.5	23 36.3	1 29.8	21 25.6	6 38.2	24R 45.1	29 5.8	24 27.0	28 6.4
7 F	14 55 12	6♏13 46	2R 44.7	25 1.5	2 43.2	21 59.4	6 33.6	24 45.1	29 3.5	24 25.4	28 5.4
8 Sa	15 52 23	20 30 12	2 43.7	26 30.5	3 56.6	22 33.3	6 29.1	24 44.9	29 1.2	24 23.8	28 4.4
9 Su	16 49 34	5♐ 8 59	2 40.6	28 3.3	5 10.0	23 7.3	6 24.8	24 44.6	28 58.8	24 22.2	28 3.5
10 M	17 46 46	20 5 53	2 34.9	29 39.6	6 23.5	23 41.5	6 20.6	24 44.3	28 56.5	24 20.6	28 2.5
11 Tu	18 43 57	5♑13 42	2 26.7	1♋19.5	7 36.9	24 15.7	6 16.5	24 43.8	28 54.2	24 19.0	28 1.7
12 W	19 41 8	20 22 49	2 16.7	3 2.9	8 50.4	24 50.0	6 12.7	24 43.2	28 51.8	24 17.4	28 0.8
13 Th	20 38 20	5♒22 51	2 6.1	4 49.6	10 3.9	25 24.5	6 9.0	24 42.6	28 49.4	24 15.8	27 60.0
14 F	21 35 32	20 4 20	1 56.0	6 39.4	11 17.5	25 59.0	6 5.5	24 41.8	28 47.1	24 14.2	27 59.2
15 Sa	22 32 44	4♓20 27	1 47.6	8 32.1	12 31.0	26 33.7	6 2.1	24 40.9	28 44.7	24 12.5	27 58.4
16 Su	23 29 57	18 7 40	1 41.5	10 27.6	13 44.6	27 8.5	5 58.9	24 40.0	28 42.3	24 10.9	27 57.6
17 M	24 27 10	1♈25 44	1 37.8	12 25.7	14 58.2	27 43.3	5 55.9	24 38.9	28 39.9	24 9.3	27 56.9
18 Tu	25 24 24	14 16 58	1 36.3	14 25.9	16 11.8	28 18.3	5 53.0	24 37.8	28 37.5	24 7.7	27 56.2
19 W	26 21 39	26 45 30	1 36.0	16 28.2	17 25.4	28 53.4	5 50.4	24 36.5	28 35.1	24 6.0	27 55.5
20 Th	27 18 54	8♉56 19	1 36.0	18 32.0	18 39.1	29 28.6	5 47.8	24 35.2	28 32.7	24 4.4	27 54.9
21 F	28 16 11	20 54 45	1 35.0	20 37.3	19 52.8	0♎ 3.9	5 45.5	24 33.7	28 30.3	24 2.8	27 54.3
22 Sa	29 13 28	2♊45 56	1 32.1	22 43.5	21 6.5	0 39.3	5 43.4	24 32.2	28 27.9	24 1.2	27 53.7
23 Su	0♌10 45	14 34 30	1 26.7	24 50.5	22 20.2	1 14.8	5 41.4	24 30.5	28 25.5	23 59.6	27 53.2
24 M	1 8 4	26 24 23	1 18.6	26 57.8	23 33.9	1 50.4	5 39.6	24 28.8	28 23.1	23 58.0	27 52.7
25 Tu	2 5 23	8♋18 45	1 7.9	29 5.3	24 47.7	2 26.2	5 38.0	24 27.0	28 20.7	23 56.4	27 52.2
26 W	3 2 43	20 19 53	0 55.2	1♌12.5	26 1.5	3 2.0	5 36.6	24 25.1	28 18.3	23 54.8	27 51.8
27 Th	4 0 4	2♌29 19	0 41.6	3 19.4	27 15.3	3 37.9	5 35.4	24 23.1	28 15.9	23 53.2	27 51.4
28 F	4 57 26	14 48 1	0 28.2	5 25.6	28 29.1	4 13.9	5 34.3	24 21.0	28 13.5	23 51.6	27 51.0
29 Sa	5 54 48	27 16 32	0 16.2	7 31.0	29 43.0	4 50.0	5 33.5	24 18.8	28 11.1	23 50.0	27 50.6
30 Su	6 52 10	9♍55 23	0 6.4	9 35.4	0♌56.8	5 26.2	5 32.8	24 16.5	28 8.7	23 48.4	27 50.3
31 M	7 49 34	22 45 16	29♎59.5	11 38.7	2 10.7	6 2.6	5 32.3	24 14.1	28 6.4	23 46.8	27 50.0

LONGITUDE AUGUST 1995

Day	☉	Noon ☽	True ☊	☿	♀	♂	♃	♄	♅	♆	♇
1 Tu	8♌46 58	5♎47 16	29♎55.6	13♌40.7	3♌24.6	6♎39.0	5♐32.0	24♓11.7	28♑ 4.0	23♑45.3	27♏49.8
2 W	9 44 22	19 2 50	29R 54.0	15 41.3	4 38.5	7 15.5	5D 31.8	24R 9.1	28R 1.7	23R 43.7	27R 49.5
3 Th	10 41 48	2♏33 44	29D 53.9	17 40.6	5 52.5	7 52.1	5 31.9	24 6.5	27 59.3	23 42.2	27 49.4
4 F	11 39 14	16 21 36	29R 54.1	19 38.4	7 6.4	8 28.7	5 32.1	24 3.8	27 57.0	23 40.7	27 49.2
5 Sa	12 36 40	0♐27 18	29 53.1	21 34.7	8 20.4	9 5.5	5 32.6	24 1.0	27 54.7	23 39.1	27 49.1
6 Su	13 34 7	14 50 21	29 50.1	23 29.5	9 34.4	9 42.4	5 33.2	23 58.1	27 52.4	23 37.6	27 49.0
7 M	14 31 35	29 28 9	29 44.6	25 22.7	10 48.4	10 19.4	5 34.0	23 55.2	27 50.2	23 36.1	27 48.9
8 Tu	15 29 4	14♑15 44	29 36.6	27 14.4	12 2.4	10 56.4	5 34.9	23 52.1	27 47.9	23 34.7	27D 48.9
9 W	16 26 34	29 5 57	29 26.9	29 4.5	13 16.5	11 33.6	5 36.1	23 49.0	27 45.7	23 33.2	27 48.9
10 Th	17 24 4	13♒50 24	29 16.4	0♍53.1	14 30.5	12 10.8	5 37.4	23 45.9	27 43.4	23 31.7	27 49.0
11 F	18 21 36	28 20 50	29 6.3	2 40.2	15 44.6	12 48.1	5 39.0	23 42.6	27 41.2	23 30.3	27 49.1
12 Sa	19 19 9	12♓30 32	28 57.9	4 25.7	16 58.7	13 25.5	5 40.7	23 39.3	27 39.1	23 28.9	27 49.2
13 Su	20 16 43	26 15 15	28 51.7	6 9.7	18 12.8	14 3.0	5 42.5	23 35.9	27 36.9	23 27.5	27 49.3
14 M	21 14 18	9♈33 33	28 48.0	7 52.1	19 26.9	14 40.5	5 44.6	23 32.4	27 34.7	23 26.1	27 49.5
15 Tu	22 11 55	22 26 33	28 46.4	9 33.1	20 41.0	15 18.2	5 46.8	23 28.9	27 32.6	23 24.7	27 49.7
16 W	23 9 34	4♉57 19	28D 46.4	11 12.7	21 55.2	15 56.0	5 49.2	23 25.3	27 30.5	23 23.3	27 50.0
17 Th	24 7 13	17 10 14	28 46.9	12 50.7	23 9.4	16 33.8	5 51.8	23 21.6	27 28.5	23 22.0	27 50.2
18 F	25 4 55	29 10 22	28R 46.9	14 27.3	24 23.6	17 11.7	5 54.6	23 17.9	27 26.4	23 20.7	27 50.6
19 Sa	26 2 38	11♊ 2 59	28 45.5	16 2.4	25 37.8	17 49.7	5 57.5	23 14.1	27 24.4	23 19.4	27 50.9
20 Su	27 0 23	22 53 13	28 42.1	17 36.1	26 52.1	18 27.8	6 0.6	23 10.2	27 22.4	23 18.1	27 51.3
21 M	27 58 9	4♋45 42	28 36.4	19 8.4	28 6.4	19 6.0	6 3.9	23 6.3	27 20.4	23 16.8	27 51.7
22 Tu	28 55 57	16 44 23	28 28.6	20 39.1	29 20.6	19 44.3	6 7.4	23 2.4	27 18.5	23 15.5	27 52.2
23 W	29 53 47	28 52 25	28 19.1	22 8.4	0♍34.9	20 22.7	6 11.0	22 58.3	27 16.6	23 14.3	27 52.6
24 Th	0♍51 38	11♌11 55	28 8.7	23 36.3	1 49.2	21 1.1	6 14.8	22 54.3	27 14.7	23 13.1	27 53.2
25 F	1 49 30	23 44 7	27 58.5	25 2.7	3 3.6	21 39.7	6 18.8	22 50.2	27 12.9	23 11.9	27 53.7
26 Sa	2 47 25	6♍29 21	27 49.2	26 27.5	4 17.9	22 18.3	6 22.9	22 46.0	27 11.0	23 10.8	27 54.3
27 Su	3 45 20	19 27 18	27 41.8	27 50.9	5 32.3	22 57.0	6 27.2	22 41.8	27 9.2	23 9.6	27 54.9
28 M	4 43 17	2♎37 20	27 36.8	29 12.7	6 46.7	23 35.8	6 31.7	22 37.5	27 7.5	23 8.5	27 55.6
29 Tu	5 41 16	15 58 43	27 34.1	0♎32.9	8 1.0	24 14.7	6 36.4	22 33.2	27 5.8	23 7.4	27 56.2
30 W	6 39 16	29 30 56	27D 33.5	1 51.4	9 15.4	24 53.7	6 41.2	22 28.9	27 4.1	23 6.3	27 57.0
31 Th	7 37 17	13♏13 43	27 34.2	3 8.3	10 29.9	25 32.7	6 46.1	22 24.5	27 2.5	23 5.3	27 57.7

*Giving the positions of planets daily at noon, in LONGITUDE Greenwich Mean Time

NOON EPHEMERIS: GMT*

SEPTEMBER 1995

Day	☉	Noon ☽	True ☊	☿	♀	♂	♃	♄	♅	♆	♇
1 F	8♍35 20	27♏ 6 57	27♎35.2	4♎23.4	11♍44.3	26♎11.8	6♐51.3	22♓20.1	27♑ 0.8	23♑ 4.3	27♏58.5
2 Sa	9 33 24	11♐10 20	27R 35.6	5 36.8	12 58.7	26 51.0	6 56.5	22R 15.7	26R 59.3	23R 3.3	27 59.3
3 Su	10 31 29	25 23 2	27 34.5	6 48.2	14 13.1	27 30.3	7 2.0	22 11.2	26 57.7	23 2.3	28 0.2
4 M	11 29 36	9♑43 7	27 31.6	7 57.7	15 27.6	28 9.7	7 7.6	22 6.8	26 56.3	23 1.3	28 1.1
5 Tu	12 27 44	24 7 26	27 26.8	9 5.2	16 42.1	28 49.1	7 13.3	22 2.2	26 54.8	23 0.4	28 2.0
6 W	13 25 54	8♒31 31	27 20.7	10 10.4	17 56.5	29 28.7	7 19.2	21 57.7	26 53.4	22 59.5	28 2.9
7 Th	14 24 5	22 50 0	27 13.9	11 13.4	19 11.0	0♏ 8.3	7 25.3	21 53.2	26 52.0	22 58.7	28 3.9
8 F	15 22 18	6♓57 21	27 7.5	12 14.0	20 25.5	0 47.9	7 31.5	21 48.6	26 50.7	22 57.8	28 4.9
9 Sa	16 20 32	20 48 41	27 2.1	13 12.0	21 40.0	1 27.7	7 37.8	21 44.0	26 49.4	22 57.0	28 5.9
10 Su	17 18 48	4♈20 29	26 58.4	14 7.3	22 54.5	2 7.5	7 44.3	21 39.4	26 48.1	22 56.2	28 7.0
11 M	18 17 6	17 31 0	26 56.4	14 59.7	24 9.0	2 47.4	7 51.0	21 34.8	26 46.9	22 55.5	28 8.1
12 Tu	19 15 27	0♉20 21	26D 56.2	15 49.0	25 23.5	3 27.4	7 57.8	21 30.2	26 45.7	22 54.7	28 9.2
13 W	20 13 49	12 50 21	26 57.1	16 34.9	26 38.0	4 7.5	8 4.7	21 25.6	26 44.6	22 54.0	28 10.4
14 Th	21 12 13	25 4 6	26 58.7	17 17.2	27 52.6	4 47.6	8 11.8	21 20.9	26 43.5	22 53.4	28 11.6
15 F	22 10 39	7♊ 5 44	27 0.1	17 55.8	29 7.1	5 27.9	8 19.0	21 16.3	26 42.5	22 52.7	28 12.8
16 Sa	23 9 8	18 59 55	27R 0.9	18 30.1	0♎21.7	6 8.2	8 26.3	21 11.7	26 41.5	22 52.1	28 14.1
17 Su	24 7 39	0♋51 34	27 0.6	19 0.1	1 36.3	6 48.6	8 33.8	21 7.1	26 40.5	22 51.5	28 15.4
18 M	25 6 12	12 45 37	26 59.0	19 25.3	2 50.9	7 29.0	8 41.4	21 2.5	26 39.6	22 51.0	28 16.7
19 Tu	26 4 47	24 46 39	26 56.1	19 45.3	4 5.5	8 9.6	8 49.2	20 57.8	26 38.8	22 50.5	28 18.0
20 W	27 3 24	6♌58 41	26 52.2	19 59.9	5 20.1	8 50.2	8 57.1	20 53.3	26 38.0	22 50.0	28 19.4
21 Th	28 2 3	19 24 57	26 47.7	20 8.6	6 34.7	9 30.9	9 5.1	20 48.7	26 37.2	22 49.5	28 20.8
22 F	29 0 45	2♍ 7 38	26 43.2	20R 11.1	7 49.3	10 11.7	9 13.2	20 44.1	26 36.5	22 49.1	28 22.2
23 Sa	29 59 28	15 7 44	26 39.1	20 7.0	9 3.9	10 52.6	9 21.5	20 39.6	26 35.8	22 48.7	28 23.7
24 Su	0♎58 14	28 25 2	26 35.9	19 56.0	10 18.6	11 33.5	9 29.9	20 35.0	26 35.2	22 48.3	28 25.2
25 M	1 57 1	11♎58 11	26 33.9	19 37.8	11 33.2	12 14.5	9 38.4	20 30.5	26 34.6	22 48.0	28 26.7
26 Tu	2 55 51	25 44 59	26D 33.2	19 12.3	12 47.9	12 55.6	9 47.1	20 26.1	26 34.1	22 47.7	28 28.2
27 W	3 54 42	9♏42 38	26 33.5	18 39.5	14 2.5	13 36.8	9 55.8	20 21.6	26 33.6	22 47.4	28 29.8
28 Th	4 53 35	23 48 10	26 34.5	17 59.3	15 17.2	14 18.0	10 4.7	20 17.2	26 33.2	22 47.2	28 31.4
29 F	5 52 30	7♐58 45	26 35.7	17 12.1	16 31.8	14 59.4	10 13.7	20 12.8	26 32.8	22 47.0	28 33.0
30 Sa	6 51 27	22 11 44	26 36.6	16 18.5	17 46.5	15 40.8	10 22.9	20 8.5	26 32.5	22 46.8	28 34.6

LONGITUDE

OCTOBER 1995

Day	☉	Noon ☽	True ☊	☿	♀	♂	♃	♄	♅	♆	♇
1 Su	7♎50 26	6♑24 43	26♎37.0	15♎19.1	19♎ 1.1	16♏22.2	10♐32.1	20♓ 4.2	26♑32.2	22♑46.7	28♏36.3
2 M	8 49 26	20 35 29	26R 36.6	14R 15.1	20 15.8	17 3.8	10 41.5	19R 59.9	26R 32.0	22R 46.6	28 38.0
3 Tu	9 48 28	4♒41 50	26 35.4	13 7.7	21 30.4	17 45.4	10 50.9	19 55.7	26 31.8	22 46.5	28 39.7
4 W	10 47 32	18 41 28	26 33.8	11 58.6	22 45.1	18 27.1	11 0.5	19 51.6	26 31.7	22 46.5	28 41.5
5 Th	11 46 37	2♓32 2	26 31.8	10 49.5	23 59.8	19 8.8	11 10.2	19 47.4	26 31.6	22D 46.5	28 43.2
6 F	12 45 44	16 11 14	26 30.0	9 42.2	25 14.4	19 50.7	11 20.0	19 43.4	26D 31.6	22 46.5	28 45.0
7 Sa	13 44 54	29 37 0	26 28.6	8 38.6	26 29.1	20 32.6	11 29.9	19 39.3	26 31.6	22 46.6	28 46.8
8 Su	14 44 5	12♈47 45	26 27.8	7 40.6	27 43.7	21 14.5	11 39.8	19 35.4	26 31.7	22 46.6	28 48.7
9 M	15 43 18	25 42 37	26D 27.5	6 49.8	28 58.4	21 56.6	11 49.9	19 31.5	26 31.8	22 46.8	28 50.5
10 Tu	16 42 33	8♉21 38	26 27.8	6 7.5	0♏13.1	22 38.7	12 0.1	19 27.6	26 32.0	22 46.9	28 52.4
11 W	17 41 51	20 45 45	26 28.4	5 34.9	1 27.7	23 20.9	12 10.4	19 23.8	26 32.2	22 47.1	28 54.3
12 Th	18 41 10	2♊56 53	26 29.1	5 12.7	2 42.4	24 3.2	12 20.8	19 20.1	26 32.5	22 47.4	28 56.2
13 F	19 40 32	14 57 50	26 29.8	5 1.3	3 57.0	24 45.5	12 31.3	19 16.4	26 32.8	22 47.6	28 58.2
14 Sa	20 39 57	26 52 7	26 30.4	5D 1.0	5 11.7	25 27.9	12 41.9	19 12.8	26 33.2	22 47.9	29 0.1
15 Su	21 39 23	8♋43 51	26 30.7	5 11.4	6 26.4	26 10.4	12 52.6	19 9.3	26 33.6	22 48.2	29 2.1
16 M	22 38 52	20 37 29	26R 30.8	5 32.3	7 41.1	26 52.9	13 3.3	19 5.8	26 34.1	22 48.6	29 4.1
17 Tu	23 38 23	2♌37 44	26 30.8	6 3.2	8 55.7	27 35.5	13 14.2	19 2.4	26 34.6	22 49.0	29 6.2
18 W	24 37 57	14 49 11	26 30.7	6 43.3	10 10.4	28 18.2	13 25.2	18 59.1	26 35.2	22 49.4	29 8.2
19 Th	25 37 32	27 16 5	26D 30.7	7 31.8	11 25.1	29 1.0	13 36.2	18 55.9	26 35.8	22 49.9	29 10.3
20 F	26 37 10	10♍ 1 59	26 30.8	8 28.0	12 39.8	29 43.8	13 47.3	18 52.7	26 36.5	22 50.4	29 12.3
21 Sa	27 36 50	23 9 23	26 31.0	9 31.0	13 54.5	0♐26.8	13 58.5	18 49.6	26 37.3	22 50.9	29 14.4
22 Su	28 36 32	6♎39 16	26 31.2	10 40.0	15 9.2	1 9.7	14 9.8	18 46.6	26 38.1	22 51.5	29 16.5
23 M	29 36 17	20 30 53	26R 31.4	11 54.3	16 23.8	1 52.8	14 21.2	18 43.7	26 38.9	22 52.1	29 18.7
24 Tu	0♏36 3	4♏41 35	26 31.4	13 13.2	17 38.5	2 35.9	14 32.6	18 40.8	26 39.8	22 52.7	29 20.8
25 W	1 35 52	19 7 0	26 31.1	14 35.9	18 53.2	3 19.1	14 44.2	18 38.1	26 40.7	22 53.4	29 23.0
26 Th	2 35 42	3♐41 27	26 30.5	16 1.9	20 7.9	4 2.4	14 55.8	18 35.4	26 41.7	22 54.1	29 25.2
27 F	3 35 34	18 18 42	26 29.6	17 30.6	21 22.6	4 45.7	15 7.5	18 32.8	26 42.8	22 54.8	29 27.3
28 Sa	4 35 28	2♑52 43	26 28.7	19 1.5	22 37.3	5 29.1	15 19.3	18 30.3	26 43.9	22 55.6	29 29.6
29 Su	5 35 24	17 18 27	26 27.9	20 34.3	23 52.0	6 12.6	15 31.1	18 27.9	26 45.0	22 56.4	29 31.8
30 M	6 35 21	1♒32 13	26D 27.5	22 8.6	25 6.6	6 56.1	15 43.0	18 25.6	26 46.2	22 57.2	29 34.0
31 Tu	7 35 20	15 31 45	26 27.6	23 44.1	26 21.3	7 39.7	15 55.0	18 23.4	26 47.4	22 58.0	29 36.2

*Giving the positions of planets daily at noon, in LONGITUDE Greenwich Mean Time

NOON EPHEMERIS: GMT* — NOVEMBER 1995

Day	☉	Noon ☽	True ☊	☿	♀	♂	♃	♄	♅	♆	♇
1 W	8♏35 20	29♒16 6	26♎28.3	25♎20.4	27♏36.0	8♐23.3	16♐ 7.0	18♓21.3	26♑48.7	22♑58.9	29♏38.5
2 Th	9 35 22	12♓45 15	26 29.4	26 57.5	28 50.6	9 7.1	16 19.1	18R 19.2	26 50.1	22 59.9	29 40.8
3 F	10 35 25	25 59 43	26 30.7	28 35.0	0♐ 5.3	9 50.8	16 31.3	18 17.3	26 51.4	23 0.8	29 43.0
4 Sa	11 35 30	9♈ 0 21	26 31.8	0♏12.9	1 19.9	10 34.7	16 43.5	18 15.5	26 52.9	23 1.8	29 45.3
5 Su	12 35 37	21 48 0	26R 32.4	1 51.0	2 34.6	11 18.6	16 55.8	18 13.7	26 54.3	23 2.8	29 47.6
6 M	13 35 46	4♉23 33	26 32.2	3 29.2	3 49.2	12 2.6	17 8.2	18 12.1	26 55.9	23 3.9	29 49.9
7 Tu	14 35 56	16 47 53	26 31.0	5 7.4	5 3.8	12 46.6	17 20.6	18 10.5	26 57.4	23 4.9	29 52.2
8 W	15 36 8	29 2 0	26 28.8	6 45.5	6 18.5	13 30.7	17 33.1	18 9.1	26 59.1	23 6.0	29 54.6
9 Th	16 36 22	11♊ 7 14	26 25.7	8 23.5	7 33.1	14 14.9	17 45.6	18 7.8	27 0.7	23 7.2	29 56.9
10 F	17 36 38	23 5 17	26 22.1	10 1.4	8 47.7	14 59.1	17 58.2	18 6.5	27 2.4	23 8.3	29 59.2
11 Sa	18 36 56	4♋58 26	26 18.2	11 39.1	10 2.3	15 43.4	18 10.8	18 5.4	27 4.2	23 9.5	0♐ 1.6
12 Su	19 37 16	16 49 31	26 14.8	13 16.5	11 16.9	16 27.7	18 23.5	18 4.3	27 6.0	23 10.8	0 3.9
13 M	20 37 38	28 42 2	26 12.0	14 53.7	12 31.5	17 12.1	18 36.3	18 3.4	27 7.9	23 12.0	0 6.3
14 Tu	21 38 1	10♌40 1	26 10.3	16 30.7	13 46.1	17 56.6	18 49.1	18 2.6	27 9.7	23 13.3	0 8.7
15 W	22 38 26	22 47 53	26D 9.8	18 7.4	15 0.7	18 41.1	19 1.9	18 1.9	27 11.7	23 14.6	0 11.0
16 Th	23 38 54	5♍10 20	26 10.4	19 43.8	16 15.3	19 25.7	19 14.8	18 1.2	27 13.7	23 16.0	0 13.4
17 F	24 39 23	17 51 54	26 11.8	21 20.0	17 29.9	20 10.4	19 27.7	18 0.7	27 15.7	23 17.3	0 15.8
18 Sa	25 39 54	0♎56 36	26 13.5	22 56.0	18 44.5	20 55.1	19 40.7	18 0.3	27 17.8	23 18.7	0 18.2
19 Su	26 40 26	14 27 17	26 14.9	24 31.7	19 59.1	21 39.9	19 53.8	17 60.0	27 19.9	23 20.2	0 20.5
20 M	27 41 1	28 25 2	26R 15.3	26 7.1	21 13.7	22 24.7	20 6.8	17 59.8	27 22.0	23 21.6	0 22.9
21 Tu	28 41 37	12♏48 26	26 14.2	27 42.4	22 28.3	23 9.6	20 19.9	17D 59.7	27 24.2	23 23.1	0 25.3
22 W	29 42 15	27 33 13	26 11.6	29 17.4	23 42.9	23 54.6	20 33.1	17 59.7	27 26.4	23 24.6	0 27.7
23 Th	0♐42 54	12♐32 22	26 7.4	0♐52.2	24 57.5	24 39.6	20 46.3	17 59.9	27 28.7	23 26.1	0 30.1
24 F	1 43 35	27 36 52	26 2.1	2 26.9	26 12.0	25 24.7	20 59.5	18 0.1	27 31.0	23 27.7	0 32.5
25 Sa	2 44 17	12♑37 8	25 56.6	4 1.4	27 26.6	26 9.8	21 12.8	18 0.4	27 33.4	23 29.3	0 34.9
26 Su	3 45 0	27 24 35	25 51.7	5 35.7	28 41.2	26 55.0	21 26.1	18 0.9	27 35.8	23 30.9	0 37.3
27 M	4 45 45	11♒52 53	25 47.9	7 9.9	29 55.7	27 40.3	21 39.4	18 1.4	27 38.2	23 32.5	0 39.7
28 Tu	5 46 30	25 58 30	25 45.8	8 44.0	1♑10.2	28 25.6	21 52.8	18 2.1	27 40.7	23 34.2	0 42.0
29 W	6 47 16	9♓40 33	25D 45.4	10 18.0	2 24.7	29 10.9	22 6.1	18 2.9	27 43.2	23 35.9	0 44.4
30 Th	7 48 3	23 0 14	25 46.4	11 51.9	3 39.2	29 56.3	22 19.6	18 3.8	27 45.7	23 37.6	0 46.8

LONGITUDE — DECEMBER 1995

Day	☉	Noon ☽	True ☊	☿	♀	♂	♃	♄	♅	♆	♇
1 F	8♐48 51	6♈ 0 3	25♎47.9	13♐25.7	4♑53.7	0♑41.7	22♐33.0	18♓ 4.7	27♑48.3	23♑39.3	0♐49.2
2 Sa	9 49 40	18 43 3	25 49.1	14 59.4	6 8.2	1 27.2	22 46.5	18 5.8	27 50.9	23 41.0	0 51.5
3 Su	10 50 29	1♉12 23	25R 49.2	16 33.1	7 22.7	2 12.8	22 59.9	18 7.0	27 53.6	23 42.8	0 53.9
4 M	11 51 20	13 30 52	25 47.3	18 6.8	8 37.1	2 58.4	23 13.4	18 8.3	27 56.3	23 44.6	0 56.2
5 Tu	12 52 12	25 40 50	25 43.0	19 40.4	9 51.6	3 44.0	23 27.0	18 9.7	27 59.0	23 46.4	0 58.6
6 W	13 53 5	7♊44 11	25 36.4	21 14.0	11 6.0	4 29.7	23 40.5	18 11.2	28 1.7	23 48.2	1 0.9
7 Th	14 53 59	19 42 26	25 27.6	22 47.6	12 20.4	5 15.5	23 54.1	18 12.9	28 4.5	23 50.1	1 3.3
8 F	15 54 54	1♋36 57	25 17.5	24 21.1	13 34.8	6 1.3	24 7.7	18 14.6	28 7.3	23 52.0	1 5.6
9 Sa	16 55 50	13 29 10	25 6.8	25 54.7	14 49.1	6 47.1	24 21.3	18 16.4	28 10.2	23 53.9	1 7.9
10 Su	17 56 47	25 20 49	24 56.6	27 28.2	16 3.5	7 33.0	24 34.9	18 18.3	28 13.0	23 55.8	1 10.3
11 M	18 57 45	7♌14 9	24 47.8	29 1.8	17 17.8	8 18.9	24 48.5	18 20.4	28 15.9	23 57.7	1 12.6
12 Tu	19 58 44	19 12 0	24 40.9	0♑35.3	18 32.1	9 4.9	25 2.2	18 22.5	28 18.9	23 59.7	1 14.9
13 W	20 59 44	1♍17 57	24 36.5	2 8.7	19 46.5	9 50.9	25 15.8	18 24.7	28 21.8	24 1.6	1 17.1
14 Th	22 0 45	13 36 7	24 34.5	3 42.1	21 0.7	10 37.0	25 29.5	18 27.1	28 24.8	24 3.6	1 19.4
15 F	23 1 47	26 11 7	24D 34.2	5 15.3	22 15.0	11 23.1	25 43.1	18 29.5	28 27.8	24 5.6	1 21.7
16 Sa	24 2 50	9♎ 7 34	24 34.9	6 48.5	23 29.3	12 9.3	25 56.8	18 32.0	28 30.9	24 7.7	1 23.9
17 Su	25 3 55	22 29 41	24R 35.5	8 21.4	24 43.5	12 55.5	26 10.5	18 34.7	28 34.0	24 9.7	1 26.2
18 M	26 5 0	6♏20 21	24 34.7	9 54.1	25 57.7	13 41.8	26 24.2	18 37.4	28 37.1	24 11.7	1 28.4
19 Tu	27 6 6	20 40 20	24 31.8	11 26.5	27 11.9	14 28.1	26 37.9	18 40.3	28 40.2	24 13.8	1 30.6
20 W	28 7 13	5♐27 14	24 26.3	12 58.4	28 26.1	15 14.5	26 51.6	18 43.2	28 43.3	24 15.9	1 32.8
21 Th	29 8 20	20 35 2	24 18.4	14 29.9	29 40.3	16 0.8	27 5.3	18 46.2	28 46.5	24 18.0	1 35.0
22 F	0♑ 9 29	5♑54 19	24 8.7	16 0.7	0♒54.4	16 47.3	27 19.0	18 49.4	28 49.7	24 20.1	1 37.2
23 Sa	1 10 37	21 13 35	23 58.2	17 30.7	2 8.5	17 33.8	27 32.7	18 52.6	28 52.9	24 22.2	1 39.3
24 Su	2 11 46	6♒21 21	23 48.4	18 59.8	3 22.6	18 20.3	27 46.3	18 55.9	28 56.2	24 24.4	1 41.5
25 M	3 12 55	21 8 13	23 40.2	20 27.6	4 36.7	19 6.8	28 0.0	18 59.3	28 59.4	24 26.5	1 43.6
26 Tu	4 14 4	5♓28 13	23 34.3	21 54.1	5 50.7	19 53.4	28 13.7	19 2.8	29 2.7	24 28.7	1 45.7
27 W	5 15 13	19 19 6	23 31.1	23 18.8	7 4.7	20 40.0	28 27.4	19 6.4	29 6.0	24 30.8	1 47.8
28 Th	6 16 22	2♈41 46	23D 30.0	24 41.4	8 18.7	21 26.7	28 41.0	19 10.1	29 9.3	24 33.0	1 49.8
29 F	7 17 31	15 39 17	23 30.1	26 1.7	9 32.6	22 13.4	28 54.6	19 13.9	29 12.6	24 35.2	1 51.9
30 Sa	8 18 40	28 15 52	23R 30.2	27 19.0	10 46.5	23 0.1	29 8.3	19 17.7	29 16.0	24 37.4	1 53.9
31 Su	9 19 49	10♉36 8	23 29.1	28 32.9	12 0.3	23 46.8	29 21.9	19 21.7	29 19.3	24 39.6	1 55.9

*Giving the positions of planets daily at noon, in LONGITUDE Greenwich Mean Time

January - Januar - janvier - enero

Monday	Tuesday	Wednesday	Thursday	Friday	Saturday	Sunday
	INANNA					1
2	3	4	5	6	7	8
9	10	11	12	13	14	15
16	17	18	19	20	21	22
23 / 30	24 / 31	25	26	27	28	29

February - Februar - fevrier - febrero

Monday	Tuesday	Wednesday	Thursday	Friday	Saturday	Sunday
		1	2	3	4	5
6	7	8	9	10	11	12
13	14	15	16	17	18	19
20	21	22	23	24	25	26
27	28					

FREYA

March - Marz - mars - marzo

Monday	Tuesday	Wednesday	Thursday	Friday	Saturday	Sunday
		1	2	3	4	5
6	7	8	9	10	11	12
13	14	15	16	17	18	19
20	21	22	23	24	25	26
27	28	29	30	31	PELE	

April - April - avril - abril

TARA

Monday	Tuesday	Wednesday	Thursday	Friday	Saturday	Sunday
					1	2
3	4	5	6	7	8	9
10	11	12	13	14	15	16
17	18	19	20	21	22	23
24	25	26	27	28	29	30

May - Mai - mai - mayo

Monday	Tuesday	Wednesday	Thursday	Friday	Saturday	Sunday
1	2	3	4	5	6	7
8	9	10	11	12	13	14
15	16	17	18	19	20	21
22	23	24	25	26	27	28
29	30	31		SAPPHO		

June - Juni - juin - junio

Monday	Tuesday	Wednesday	Thursday	Friday	Saturday	Sunday
			1	2	3	4
5	6	7	8	9	10	11
12	13	14	15	16	17	18
19	20	21	22	23	24	25
26	27	28	29	30	KWAN-YIN	

July - Juli - juiliet - julio

Monday	Tuesday	Wednesday	Thursday	Friday	Saturday	Sunday
		OSHUN			1	2
3	4	5	6	7	8	9
10	11	12	13	14	15	16
17	18	19	20	21	22	23
24 / 31	25	26	27	28	29	30

August - August - aout - agosto

Monday	Tuesday	Wednesday	Thursday	Friday	Saturday	Sunday
	1	2	3	4	5	6
7	8	9	10	11	12	13
14	15	16	17	18	19	20
21	22	23	24	25	26	27
28	29	30	31			

ARTEMIS

September - septembre - septiembre

Monday	Tuesday	Wednesday	Thursday	Friday	Saturday	Sunday
		ISIS		1	2	3
4	5	6	7	8	9	10
11	12	13	14	15	16	17
18	19	20	21	22	23	24
25	26	27	28	29	30	

October - Oktober - octobre - octubre

KALI

Monday	Tuesday	Wednesday	Thursday	Friday	Saturday	Sunday
						1
2	3	4	5	6	7	8
9	10	11	12	13	14	15
16	17	18	19	20	21	22
23 / 30	24 / 31	25	26	27	28	29

November - novembre - noviembre

Monday	Tuesday	Wednesday	Thursday	Friday	Saturday	Sunday
		1	2	3	4	5
6	7	8	9	10	11	12
13	14	15	16	17	18	19
20	21	22	23	24	25	26
27	28	29	30			

BUFFALO WOMAN

December - decembre - diciembre

Monday	Tuesday	Wednesday	Thursday	Friday	Saturday	Sunday
LILLITH				1	2	3
4	5	6	7	8	9	10
11	12	13	14	15	16	17
18	19	20	21	22	23	24
25	26	27	28	29	30	31